Weathering the Storm

Weathering the Storm

Simple Strategies for Being Peaceful and Prepared

TRACY W. MEHR-MUSKA

RESOURCE *Publications* • Eugene, Oregon

WEATHERING THE STORM
Simple Strategies for Being Peaceful and Prepared

Resource Publications
An Imprint of Wipf and Stock Publishers
199 W. 8th Ave., Suite 3
Eugene, OR 97401

www.wipfandstock.com

PAPERBACK ISBN: 978-1-5326-5237-0
HARDCOVER ISBN: 978-1-5326-5238-7
EBOOK ISBN: 978-1-5326-5239-4

Manufactured in the U.S.A.   APRIL 10, 2019

To Scott, Noah, and Elsie, who inspire me to try to be my best self
and forgive me when I fall short.

And to the many resilient people I have encountered
who have shown me how to persevere.

Contents

Permissions

Excerpt of lyrics from "Seize the Day" are from *Clearwater* by Chris and Meredith Thompson, copyright © 2002 Chris and Meredith Thompson. Used by permission. All rights reserved.

Scripture quotations marked NRSV are taken from the New Revised Standard Version Bible, copyright © 1989 National Council of the Churches of Christ in the United States of America. Used by permission. All rights reserved worldwide.

Scripture quotations marked NIV are taken from the New International Version®, copyright © 1973, 1978, 1984, 2011 by Biblica, Inc.™ Used by permission of Zondervan. All rights reserved worldwide. www.zondervan.com.

Scripture quotations marked GNT are taken from the Good News Bible, copyright © 1994 published by the Bible Societies/HarperCollins Publishers Ltd UK, Good News Bible © American Bible Society 1966, 1971, 1976, 1992. Used with permission.

Quotation by Fred Rogers was taken from his commencement speech given at Marquette University, copyright © 2001 Fred Rogers. Used by permission of Family Communications Inc. All rights reserved.

The stories about the author's classmates were used by permission and were derived from personal experiences, email exchanges, and interviews, and all stories shared are true to the best of our knowledge.

Acknowledgements

I AM OVERFLOWING WITH gratitude. My husband, Scott, and my children, Noah and Elsie, were incredibly patient and supportive during this process of study, research, and writing. Members of my family of origin—Rob, Peg, and Megan Mehr—have been unconditionally loving and have given me the gifts of curiosity, grit, and belonging. My female-identified Coast Guard Academy classmates whose stories I highlight demonstrated such enthusiasm, generosity, and bravery in sharing their testimonies of resilience and flourishing for this book, and many other academy classmates and Coast Guard shipmates—those cited and unmentioned, male and female, officer and enlisted—helped shape who I have become, laughed with me when laughing was our only alternative, and showed me how to be sturdy and determined. The wisdom and compassion of the Rev. Robert Dykstra and my spiritual director, Joanne White, helped lead me to a healthier understanding of my experiences and a deeper appreciation for myself as a person. Scott Thumma and the Rev. Donna Schaper helped me turn my curiosity about resilience into a ministry project and ultimately into this book. My husband Scott, Victoria Pitts-Taylor, and John Merz helped edit this book and engaged in rich and meaningful conversations with me that grew out of their questions. My church small group has consistently cheered me on and urged me to believe in myself. My colleagues at Wesleyan University supported and encouraged my study of resilience and provided valuable feedback and inspiration, specifically Rabbi David Teva, Imam Sami Aziz, Imam Adeel Zeb, Jennifer D'Andrea, Laura Patey, David Phillips, Tanya Purdy, and the Rev. Jenny Peek. Each of these individuals, and many more whom I have not mentioned here, made this project possible.

I am also grateful to the many strong, magnificent, gritty people I served in ministry and for the many moments of grace I witnessed that have helped me reflect on resilience and have inspired me to work on cultivating my own resilience every day. Most importantly, I give thanks to the Divine, upon whose companionship and unconditional love I have depended when doors have closed and when hope seemed lost.

The Characteristics of Resilience

The quality of strength lined with tenderness is an unbeatable combination.

—MAYA ANGELOU[1]

PREPARING THE SHIP FOR SEA is a sailor's priority. Those who go to sea follow practices and procedures methodically when the ship is safely in port to make the ship resilient against approaching storms. The crew trains for different emergencies such as flooding and fires to ensure they are well prepared and have essential equipment. The sailors ensure the ship is stocked with emergency beacons, flairs, and radios in case they are needed, and they strictly utilize the watertight doors and conduct thorough safety inspections multiple times a day. They spend most of their time preparing and drilling for the worst case scenarios, hoping they will never come. Sailors understand that this preparation must be done in advance. They also know that in heavy seas, even properly secured ships will absorb damage, maybe needing some repairs at the end of the voyage, but well-prepared sailors go to sea confident that the ship will return to port regardless of what they encounter.

Securing a ship for stormy seas is a helpful analogy for the ways we can prepare to navigate the stormy seas of life. The resilience that we need in order to withstand hardship and trauma doesn't passively develop itself, and it is not something we are born with. Instead, resilience is a set of characteristics that we have the power to cultivate. This book provides us with some research-based practices, strategies, exercises, and examples that will enable us to identify and develop these essential characteristics. We will

1. Angelou, *I Know Why*, 115.

emerge more buoyant and better prepared for the difficulties, disappointments, and unwanted changes that we will inevitably face. This book *will* make us more seaworthy and give us the ability and confidence to weather life's storms.

As a Presbyterian minister serving as a university chaplain, I can't avoid the subject of resilience, and most of my job involves helping my students build it. In some cases, the ways that I do that as a college chaplain are obvious. I prayerfully sit with my students and listen as they share their complicated struggles and, in some cases, profound suffering, wiping their tears of grief and lament and quietly offering support and encouragement. I aim to help them see the ways in which their faith or belief systems can be sources of comfort and strength by inviting them to share about their spiritual or religious views and their sources of spiritual support. I struggle to help them grow closer to the Holy during a time when society is relentlessly pulling them away from all that is sacred.

But I am also helping them build resilience in less obvious ways. I help students develop leadership and problem-solving skills, and I spend hours talking with them about their senses of purpose and vocational callings as they wrestle with decisions related to course selection, grad school, and even organic chemistry. I provide them with nonjudgmental emotional support while they confess and reflect upon their transgressions, regrets, and bad choices, and I invite them to embrace a spirit of flexibility as they face the many wanted and unwanted changes college life presents. I connect them with encouraging people on and off campus who can help them personally and professionally. I drink *a lot* of coffee, pick apples, baptize, lead retreats, do crafts, hammer nails, visit the psychiatric unit at the hospital, fearfully scale the aerial ropes course, serve communion, drive vans, watch movies, and eat a lot of Indian food—a crowd favorite. All of these interventions, from the most sacred to the most mundane, are helping us all become more resilient.

With the world as wild as it seems now, we all need some extra resilience. Indicators show that we are now more vulnerable and less buoyant. Among young adults, for instance, nearly a quarter of college students reported experiencing overwhelming anxiety, and over one in ten considered suicide.[2] Young adults are smoking, drinking, vaping, and taking illegal drugs at alarming rates. We are all facing a world that is increasingly competitive, complex, and hostile. This is a time of social, economic,

---

2. "American College Health Association," 33.

and political polarization and uncertainty, and on top of that, we each will experience unexpected struggles, traumas, and unwanted changes in our lives. Authentic connections are increasingly difficult to make, and many of us are dealing with a variety of challenges such as grief and loss, unfulfilling marriages, identity issues, sexual harassment and assault, bullying, illness and injury, lack of belonging, the pressure for perfectionism and overachievement, and unfulfilling vocations where we feel underappreciated and overworked. We can all use a little more resilience to deal with life!

I am passionate about this topic because I am not a naturally resilient person. After my first exposure to violence, I realized just how unresilient I was and how much help I needed. In the early 1980s, in an effort to protect us and provide us with an untroubled childhood, my parents moved our young family from a bustling urban part of New Jersey, just a few miles from New York City, to the rural northwest part of the state, where we were greeted with pasturelands, rolling hills, and quaint historic downtowns. We biked unhelmeted up and down quiet cul-de-sacs and built forts and hideouts in the woods. It was a safe and uneventful existence.

Yet during my sophomore year of high school, I found my seat in the middle of the front row of our public speaking class and something unexpected happened. The bell had not yet rung, so my friends and I were gathering and chatting. Just then, an angry student stormed in and began to viciously attack one of my male friends in the front of the classroom. I was completely frozen and felt trapped in my seat, with a front-row view of the barbaric and relentless assault on my friend. My sheltered existence was shattered. People regularly confront violence in their homes, communities, and schools and are unfazed, but, as irrational as it may seem now, this first exposure to violence made me feel powerless, unsafe, and vulnerable.

I became stuck in a dark place of questioning and disillusionment, and I was continually fighting my fear, panic attacks, and insomnia. For a time, I was even too fragile to go to school dances and football games, and I missed out on many enjoyable events and memories. I judged my inability to cope very harshly at first, but I have come to learn and observe that people can have widely different reactions to the same type of traumatic event.[3] So if being resilient is bouncing back from difficulty or trauma, or simply "toughness," I was definitely *not* resilient. In response to the fear I was feeling related to violence and disorder, I decided a military academy would

3. Souers, *Fostering Resilient Learners*, 15.

be a good fit for me because of its discipline, predictability, and structure. Needless to say, attending a service academy did not solve my problems.

I arrived at the Coast Guard Academy on July 7, 1992, with a strong leadership résumé, feeling physically and emotionally prepared for my new haircut and my new life. What I realize now was that I also brought with me a deep dependence on affirmation and validation. Affirmation and validation were not part of the agenda of basic training, and my contact with my existing sources of support was almost completely shut off. My self-esteem and sense of identity began to erode. I internalized the harsh judgment of our squad leaders and the gender bias from some of my peers. I felt like a failure—worthless and unwelcome.

By the time I graduated and became a commissioned officer, I was emotionally run down, disconnected from my sources of support, and emotionally adrift. When I reported to my first unit, a 210-foot ship, they were expecting me to be male and did not have a berthing space for me. They welded a third rack and a small metal desk into the stateroom of the two older, close-knit female officers who had been the only women onboard. These officers were not happy to share their space with an ensign fresh out of the academy that they anticipated being hard-charging, self-important, idealistic, and naïve (to some extent, their assumptions were accurate). Needless to say, I was lonely, isolated, and lacking self-esteem. This was a dangerous combination.

Soon into my first tour, the two women transferred, and I was the only female remainingamong the crew of seventy-five. The loneliness was crushing, and one night in my homeport I was sexually assaulted by an officer senior to me whom I admired and trusted. When I discussed it with an empathetic friend soon after, I found myself trying to minimize and justify what happened to me, even after he said with intensity and compassion, "Tracy, listen—you were raped." Because of my low self-esteem and lack of mooring, I blamed myself. At that point, my desperation for validation, affirmation, belonging, and empathy was profound, and it eventually steered me into a nourishing and uplifting relationship with a young and caring chief petty officer, a hard-working man who had worked his way up quickly to the senior enlisted ranks. Rules prohibit romantic relationships between the commissioned officers and enlisted personnel, so we were reprimanded when we came forward about the relationship. The chief was slated for Officer Candidate School, but that was rescinded as part of our punishment. Because ending the relationship seemed impossible, I believed at the time that the best option was to resign my commission. Sadly, my spirit was then completely broken due to the shame I felt for having the relationship, the grief I felt for giving up a career of military service that I dreamt for myself, and the responsibility I took for damaging the status of women in the military and this dedicated sailor's career. Because of all of that, the relationship was doomed and sadly ended not long after. My life fell apart, but thankfully, that wasn't the end of the story.

It has taken me about thirty years to put to words the spiritual, emotional, and psychosocial growth that happened from the time I was a vulnerable and fragile high school sophomore to when I became a more adaptable and durable adult. I have discovered the things that have bolstered my spirit—people and perspectives that helped me rebuild my life from the teary Amtrak train ride back to my parents' home after my discharge, when I felt utterly hopeless, when I felt that my bad choices made me a bad person, to today, where I have a fulfilling ministry, amazing family, and strong sense of purpose. Thankfully, it has generally been a journey forward, but I cannot deny the setbacks along the way. Being resilient is an ongoing goal for me. Early in my ministry career, someone said that the sermons we preach are often the ones we need to hear, and I believe that is why this book is important to me. I need to continue to develop and cultivate resilience, and I'm so glad to bring you along for the journey and hope that you too will feel more peaceful and prepared for the challenges and changes that life brings.

WHAT RESILIENCE IS

We are often told that resilience is about toughness or grit. The *Titanic* was pretty tough—"unsinkable" even—but that is not why it is a household name. The idea of toughness, the "suck it up, buttercup" philosophy, is far too simplistic and one dimensional. One scholar provides a more nuanced definition or resilience, saying that it is "the set of attributes that provides people with the strength and fortitude to confront the overwhelming obstacles they are bound to face in life."[4] This definition is an improvement but misses several essential elements of resilience that are critical for a more complete understanding of it. It falls short because it seems to focus on static attributes, deemphasizes the spiritual aspect of resilience, and addresses only simply confronting or surviving hardships.

4. Sagor, "Building Resiliency," para. 3.

First, this definition describes resilience as a set of "attributes." When I think of "attributes," I think of qualities like IQ or shoe size. These are arguably inborn qualities, not necessarily aspects of ourselves that we can readily improve or strengthen. I instead use the word "characteristics." This word emphasizes the reality that resilience is *not* inborn but is instead comprised of characteristics that are based on resources, skills, and tools that we have the ability to develop and cultivate. We *can* increase our level of resilience by working on the simple characteristics of resilience that I will detail in this book.

Second, this definition doesn't acknowledge the spiritual component. Nearly 80 percent of Americans identify as spiritual and/or religious,[5] and I believe that number doesn't represent the many more who identify with issues that can be considered "spiritual," such as seeking a sense of purpose, love, and belonging. There is an essential connection between spirituality and resilience. Although the word "spiritual" may have a negative connotation to some readers, I believe resilience is a spiritual issue, and I invite you to reclaim the word for yourself and open yourself up to discovering and cultivating this association for yourself in chapter 6.

Finally, the last part of this scholar's definition—confronting obstacles—ignores a key element of resilience. To me, cultivating the characteristics of resilience enables a person to do much more than just confront obstacles. True resilience leads to the intrinsic ability for an individual to be *transformed* by pain and strife, and it invites an individual to discover increased ability, strength, self-awareness, and intention. With those reflections in mind, I define resilience as *a simple set of characteristics that can be continuously cultivated to enable people to be emotionally, cognitively, and spiritually prepared for and positively transformed by trauma, disappointment, and difficulty.*

WHAT RESILIENCE IS NOT

As I said before, resilience is *not* predetermined by our DNA. Though some individuals may seem "naturally" resilient, the characteristics of resilience that I will describe are qualities that we can cultivate and develop with mindful intention, and I feel strongly that this work is best done in advance of our facing challenges or trauma. Think of building resilience as a fire drill; we don't wait until there is a fire in our home or workplace

5. Lipka and Gecewicz, "More Americans," infographic 1.

to determine how to safely egress. We establish plans and conduct drills to ensure the safest and fastest routes are familiar. These practices empower us to escape safely, calmly, and confidently. Similarly, it is not in the middle of a crisis that we should be starting yoga practices, reaching out to mentors, or trying to change our default outlooks. These are examples, however, of practices that I will address that can become habits that will help us better prepare for potential—arguably inevitable—crises and difficulties.

So, resilience is not inborn, and it is also not about *fixing* a situation. It is not about mending our brokenness or spontaneously healing our grief, but it is, as said by Princeton Seminary professor Margarita Mooney, about "living a broken life, beautifully."[6] In doing so, there is no expectation of us denying the suffering that accompanies hardship or trauma. Experiencing the pain and grief associated with trauma or disappointment is a necessary part of healing, and it is in no way an indication of a lack of resilience. We can be both grief-stricken and resilient. We can be hurt or angry or worried and still be resilient. In fact, being self-aware and acknowledging our feelings are important components of resilience because working with and through the feelings is far more effective and helpful than denying or suppressing them. Giving ourselves permission to feel the feelings also enables us to more accurately assess our needs and to bring our strengths and resources to bear in order to be transformed.

Importantly, resilience is not something to be achieved, even though our culture and society often characterize it that way. We don't wake up one day and say, "That's it! I'm resilient now!" That said, the characteristics of resilience *can* be cultivated, understanding that there will be setbacks on the journey we take toward a place of increased strength and peace. Resilience is a continuum, and at different points in life we might find ourselves in different places on the continuum. Our place on this continuum may change, for the better or worse, based on our circumstances and lived experience, since some events and relationships that are outside of our control may work against our resilience. Still, the efforts we put into cultivating the characteristics of resilience will move us toward the stronger end of the spectrum and put us in better positions to weather the setbacks.

Although it will require effort, cultivating the characteristics of resilience is not a burden but rather a choice. It is a privilege and an opportunity that reap lifelong benefits and equip us to face difficulty, take sensible risks with more confidence and less fear, help others, endure challenges, and be

---

6. Mooney, "What Does It Mean?"

successful personally and professionally. It will help us be more responsive friends, parents, partners, children, employees, and bosses, and it will truly enable us to enjoy life more, which leads to the final point: resilience is not an entirely individual endeavor. True resilience requires more than just our individual selves and is deeply related to the connections we make with others, the inspiration we find in historical and modern-day stories of survival, and the resources we access. We are not alone on this journey.

WHAT YOU WILL ENCOUNTER IN THIS BOOK

Through research and personal and spiritual reflection, I now recognize the characteristics that have helped me be more resilient. These characteristics largely align with the common characteristics identified by researchers in their studies of resilient people.[7] In this book, I highlight these characteristics and present them in a way that I hope is helpful, unique, and memorable—the Seven Ps of Resilience:

- People
- Positivity
- Pliability
- Problem Solving
- Piety (or spirituality more broadly, but that doesn't start with P!)
- Purpose
- Perseverance

Putting effort into internalizing and growing these characteristics of resilience will help us feel more peaceful and more prepared to face the future and its possibilities.

This list of Seven Ps is not exhaustive. Just recently, my then eight-year-old daughter asked why Patience is not on the list. After a long pause, I decided that it probably should be! A Presbyterian colleague asked why Perspiration was omitted. It's also a good one! There may be additional characteristics that are relevant specifically to *you* that are not listed here.

---

7. Akhtar and Wrenn, "Biopsychosocial Miracle," 15; Boyden and Mann, "Children's Risk," 6–7; Garmenzy, "Reflections and Commentary," 14; Charney and Southwick, *Resilience*, 13.

I invite you to explore what those might be for you as you read the book. I hope that these Seven Ps are at least a good place to start.

This book is admittedly ambitious. I plan to describe these important characteristics of resilience and invite you to cultivate your resilience through the following:

First, I will share some evidence and anecdotes supporting these characteristics. Resilience is a spiritual issue since it directly relates to our sense of being, purpose, belonging, and capacity. I ground these characteristics of resilience in multifaith stories and theologies since nearly every religious or spiritual tradition is ripe with the encouragement to endure hardship and awash with role models of strength and endurance. I acknowledge that my training and ordination is exclusively in the Protestant tradition, though I share wisdom, readings, and spiritual practices from different spiritual and religious traditions. I do not intend to enable religious or cultural appropriation or generalize the beliefs of others, but, whether you identify as religious or not, I invite you to discover which religious writings, perspectives, stories, and spiritual practices speak to you most deeply while also asking you to be respectful of the sources, should you choose to incorporate them into your life and practice. You might believe that some stories I share from various sacred texts are historical or that some are mythological. Either way, I invite you to hear the stories with an openness to learning from them and being inspired by them, even if you think they're entirely mythical, just as my young self was unapologetically empowered by Lynda Carter in the early seventies (and still, since I now watch vintage *Wonder Woman* reruns with my daughter!). In addition, I quote theologians and holy writings from different traditions and chose to remain true to the original words or translations, even though these writings often use male pronouns for humankind and the Divine. I hope this is not a distraction for some readers and invite you to use pronouns that are authentic to your faith and experience, regardless of the pronouns used in this text.

Second, near the end of each chapter, I illustrate each of these characteristics using the story of a friend who exemplifies the characteristic and can serve as a role model for us. It is important to me to share stories about real people that I know and respect. These are not ultra-resilient, faultless, extra-ordinary people that I picked out of the seven billion people in this world; the examples I provide are of women I know and love that were among the three dozen caring, hard-working female classmates from the Coast Guard Academy class of 1996. As you will see, these women's stories are not necessarily related to their military service, but instead are stories of everyday people who have demonstrated each of these characteristics of resilience in beautiful and inspirational ways. These women have each been instrumental in my life and my own personal survival, from our days running the obstacle course during basic training, to serving in each other's wedding parties, to supporting each other through divorces, cross-country moves, and miscarriages. I hope you come to love these women as I do. And even though I am highlighting a tiny snapshot of only a small number of women, there are many equally resilient and incredible people whose stories are similarly beautiful, inspirational, and worthy of being told. In fact, we are all surrounded by incredible people who have endured hardship and can likewise inspire, encourage, and embolden us on our journeys of increased resilience.

Third, in each chapter, I will invite you to ask yourself challenging questions that will help you identify and celebrate your strengths and will reveal areas for growth related to each of these characteristics. You can reflect upon these questions while you journal, meditate, or converse with a friend, religious leader, counselor, or spiritual director. There are no "right" or "wrong" answers to these questions. These questions are not intended to cause you to brood over what you are lacking or obsess about the ways you are inadequate (habits that I am guilty of doing!), but they are meant to be useful questions that will help you discover areas where there is room for growth that would benefit from some mindful attention.

I will also provide some strategies that you can employ that can help reinforce each of these characteristics and move you forward on the continuum of resilience to a place of increased readiness, strength, effectiveness, and ability as you prepare yourself for the unexpected changes and difficulties that lie ahead. Just as you are unlikely to become more athletic without exercise, you are unlikely to become more resilient without being mindful of these characteristics and working on the strategies for building them. These strategies can be incorporated into your life quite easily. You can consider including these as new or revived practices for transitional holidays such as Lent, the New Year, or Rosh Hashanah, or you can take them up in cooperation with a friend or small group. I encourage you to be very intentional about incorporating these strategies; set goals for yourself that are concrete, specific, and time bound, and have strategies for accountability with a friend, small group, counselor, or faith leader.

Finally, I included a prayer at the end of each chapter. I encourage you to amend or edit this prayer to make it relevant to your belief system. If you are uncomfortable with the prayer, feel free to ignore it entirely.

ALL ABOARD!

An old proverb says that the best time to plant a tree is twenty years ago, but the *next* best time is today. Wherever you are on your journey, or however unprepared or incapable you might feel about facing an uncertain future, *now* is the *best* time to work on cultivating your resilience. My prayer for you is that this journey of cultivating your resilience is full of fun, fulfillment, and growth. I hope you will realize the many gifts, resources, and strengths you already possess and feel inspired to consciously mobilize those gifts, resources, and strengths as you experience the ups and downs of life. I hope you will learn practices and exercises that will help you feel stronger, more confident, and less fearful going forward. May it be so.

I

People

Two are better than one, because they have a good reward for their toil.
For if they fall, one will lift up the other;
but woe to one who is alone and falls
and does not have another to help.

—Ecclesiastes 4:9–10 (NRSV)

Having strong social connections to *People* is a key element of resilience. When we actively ask for help and allow ourselves to be supported, upheld, and inspired during difficult times, we can discover a sense of buoyancy when we need it most. When I served as an interfaith chaplain in a trauma hospital, I felt a deep need for our patients to see caring and encouraging familiar faces before they went into surgery or when they regained consciousness. One morning when I was on duty, the helicopter transport crew brought in an unconscious man who was in a serious car accident. As victims were brought to the trauma center, my initial task was to determine their names and notify their next of kin. His wallet was left at the scene, so I only had the bloodied employee badge clipped to his collar to use to track down his nearest family member. I rushed to the phone, desperately calling numbers related to his workplace, inching closer and closer to finding the name and number of a partner or friend. To me, it seemed impossibly unfair for him to suffer alone, without anyone who cares about him nearby. I was so relieved when I finally tracked down his wife who rushed to the hospital to be by his side. Making these connections was so important to me because I only survived the hardships in my life because of the individuals, communities, mentors, mentees, and role models who inspired, encouraged, guided, and companioned me through the difficult times.

The benefits of social connection are not just anecdotal or subjective. Scientists have proven that strong social connections are good for your health and wellness,[1] and they have discovered the specific brain processes that allow strong, healthy social connections to reduce anxiety, stress, and fear.[2] Conversely, being without such connections—being lonely—can be devastating and life-limiting. Scholars have implicated loneliness as a contributing factor in suicidal ideation among veterans of combat and captivity,[3] and the prime minister of the United Kingdom recently appointed a "minister for loneliness" who is to address the physical and social costs of loneliness through education, funding, and public policy.[4] In my work as a hospice chaplain, we would regularly observe our patients' conditions improve after coming onto hospice services, and our team believed that this was due in part to the increased social visits and emotional support we provided. Social connection is essential. Even without conclusive data to back it up, would you rather be looking for the Demogorgon in the Upside Down in *Stranger Things* alone or with a friend?

BARRIERS TO DEVELOPING SOCIAL CONNECTIONS

Before talking about the types of social connections that can help us be more resilient, it is worthwhile acknowledging what might be in the way of our making deep, meaningful social connections. First, we may not want others to see all of the imperfections, dysfunction, and sorrow that is realistically in our lives and hearts. As a college chaplain, I often hear my students voice their worry about seeming flawed and imperfect, especially in light of all the happiness and success displayed by their friends and family on social media. Even in the past few months, two adult friends expressed to me their reluctance to tell their parents of serious struggles they were

1. Holt-Lunstad et al., "Advancing Social Connection," 517.
2. Southwick and Charney, *Resilience*, 109–110.
3. Stein et al., "Traumatization," 5–6.
4. Yeginsu, "U.K. Appoints," para. 5.

facing, perhaps because they didn't want to worry them or because of a fear of being judged. For many of us, being fully open and transparent feels too risky, and we are reluctant to be fully truthful and vulnerable, even with people we know and love.

I have been trying to better tolerate my own imperfection in my life and work. Recently, I put together a program for my college students and was working with Jackson, one of my student leaders, on the finishing touches for the program. I wasn't nearly as organized as I wanted to be and confessed to my student leader, "Wow, I'd like to think I'm organized and on top of things, but this is a mess!" He laughed and said lovingly, "You're our Ms. Frizzle," referring to the scattered, quirky science teacher in the children's books series *The Magic School Bus*. He must have noticed my stunned look of offense because he went on to quickly clarify that she is not only quirky and scattered, but she is also protective, loving, encouraging, and student-centered, she takes risks for the sake of learning and community building, and she is appreciated. Okay, I thought to myself, maybe I should just embrace the persona of "The Friz," imperfect but valuable and appreciated. Wouldn't it be great if we could all reject the notions of perfection and embrace the messiness of real life? Like Professor Frizzle, we would have a lot more fun and be more resilient too!

In addition to the fear of exposing our imperfection, building strong connections can be hindered by our fear of getting a reputation for being too needy. In healthy relationships, sometimes we are the givers of support, and sometimes we are the recipients. At any given time, a relationship might feel a little imbalanced, but there is generally a give and take that stems from mutual respect and love. Recently, an old friend was working through marital challenges with her partner. During that time, we spoke and texted more frequently, often about the difficulties and grief associated with her broken relationship and family transition. I was happy to listen and provide support, and I absolutely know and trust that when—not if—I need extra calls or visits, she will be unrelentingly gracious with her time and love. There are both times when we can provide support and times when we may need some extra support.

Sadly, there are additional sociological trends working against our seeking support from other people. People now are more likely to postpone marrying and having families, and some are choosing to participate in relationships that are nonbinding or casual.[5] These trends are not inher-

---

5. Smith and Snell, *Souls in Transition*, 70 and 58.

ently harmful, but they do risk eating away at the critical social support a healthy, dependable relationship or family could provide. People also have a decreased sense of civic obligation and community involvement,[6] which are ways that we have historically found community, friendships, and belonging. As if that's not enough, there is a reported decrease in empathy and increase in depression,[7] further distancing us from connections that can help us withstand disappointment, trauma, and hardship. But even with these realities, do not despair! This characteristic of resilience can be easily developed, and we might be pleasantly surprised about how much fun we have doing it as we focus on the following: developing personal relationships with individuals, connecting with communities, participating in mentoring relationships, and discovering inspirational role models.

RELATIONSHIPS WITH INDIVIDUALS

An obvious and essential way to bolster our resilience is through one-on-one relationships with others. Having people that we trust deeply is critically important. During one of my Coast Guard deployments, for instance, we boarded a freighter suspected of smuggling drugs. My shipmate Bob and I were tasked with putting on hooded, chemical-protection "hazmat" suits with respirators and crawling into a deep, dark storage tank below decks to look for hidden compartments with the ship's crew menacingly looking on. I was nauseous, claustrophobic, and terrified. Bob and I knew each other well, so we prayed together and helped each other keep calm while we conducted the search. Our strong connection and mutual support made me more resilient, even if we did fail to find a stash of drugs that day.

These connections can sometimes be difficult to create or recognize. One Presbyterian pastor recalled an interesting conversation he had while serving as a youth pastor. He asked members of his youth group to list five people to whom they can confess absolutely *anything* and expect continued unconditional love. When some of them could not list even one person, he was feeling a little self-conscious, since he had been working very hard as their pastor to help them see *him* as that resource![8] We likely have people in our lives who would be happy to connect more deeply with us if we were to make these relationships a priority. Whether we are introverts or

---

6. Wuthnow, *After the Baby Boomers*, 38.

7. Williams, "Is Gen Y Becoming," paras. 8–9.

8. Nishioka and Robinson, "Resilience and Joy."

extroverts, having non-judgmental friends and family members is invaluable when we need to unload, confess, cry, or discern.

The important and supportive roles of our family and friends cannot be understated, but also important is the support we can receive from professionals such as psychiatrists, therapists, spiritual directors, or pastoral counselors. Several years ago, just before the New Year, I remember deeply struggling with the decision of whether or not I should move from part-time to full-time chaplaincy. I had two small kids at home and was admittedly already pretty overwhelmed. I met with my spiritual director Joanne and cerebrally detailed all the financial and professional benefits of going full time. I considered my friends who were working full time while volunteering as room parent, helping out at church, and even sewing their kids' Halloween costumes. "Well, if they could do it, I should be able to, also," I said confidently, followed by a cautious and hesitant, "Right?" After listing my reasons and rationalizing why I should say yes to the extra hours, we sat a moment in silence.

Then she quietly asked, "Tracy, what is your dream for yourself in 2015?"

I thought for a few moments, and as tears welled in my eyes, I answered, "To be a better mother."

Saying what we both knew to be true, she replied, "Well, it sounds like you might be making a decision that would work against your own dream for yourself." While I was so busy letting my ego drive my decision and using my brain to defend it, she patiently listened and helped me uncover my true needs and dreams. Remaining part time at that moment was perhaps one of the best decisions I ever made. Having an external, unbiased, trained person to listen, support, and gently guide was truly healing and life changing.

Another source of individual connection that many celebrate is the important role of pets in our resilience. Military veterans treated for Post-Traumatic Stress Disorder reported that adopting a dog helped them feel "calmer, less lonely, less depressed, and less worried about their and their family's safety."[9] The American Psychological Association found that those who owned pets enjoyed higher levels of self-esteem, physical fitness, and extraversion, while reporting lower levels of loneliness and fear than those without pets.[10] I'll certainly never forget the childlike excitement on my

9. Stern et al., "Potential Benefits," § "Findings," para. 2.

10. Mills, "Truth," para. 4.

ninety-two-year-old grandmother's face when the sweet, calming therapy dog came to visit her in her hospice house. All of these characteristics are consistent with increased resilience. Many people testify to the empathy and unconditional love pets provide, further making them an excellent source for the personal connection. Perhaps the best part is that pets are unlikely to give us bad advice!

Having strong connections with others is also essential because we all have different gifts, perspectives, and abilities. One blogger said it well: "Human civilizations rest on the specialization, differentiation, and orchestration of human expertise so that we, as a collective, can achieve more than we could by our solitary efforts."[11] We can rely upon each other and celebrate our individual gifts instead of lamenting our perceived deficiencies or shortcomings.

Moses, a hero from the Hebrew Bible, exemplifies this. When he was a baby, Moses's survival was dependent on his mother courageously hiding him and strategizing a way for him to be adopted and protected by an Egyptian princess. Then, the dedication and quick thinking of his big sister Miriam led to their mother serving as Moses's nurse. As his life and divine calling developed, Moses felt convicted to stand up against the terrible treatment and conditions that the Israelites experienced as slaves in Egypt, and he was later chosen by God to help free the Israelites. Moses was not a good public speaker and was "slow of speech and tongue."[12] At that point, his brother Aaron stepped up and served as his spokesperson. So in this one story, at least *four* other people played essential roles in the liberation of mistreated people (three of whom were women!), when Moses often gets all the credit. Moses did *not* have all of the gifts and skills he needed, but he relied on the people in his life to help encourage and assist him in fulfilling his calling. When we attempt to accomplish something alone, we are much more likely to fail, even if we firmly believe we are doing what our higher self, the universe, or God intends for us to do. We truly benefit from seeking help and being willing to receive help from those around us who have gifts and abilities that we might lack.

Bolstering our resilience with these individual connections can be either active or passive. Sometimes, our suffering is obvious, and people reach out to us to offer their love and encouragement. We simply just need to be open to receiving it. Other times, such as several months after the

11. Cacioppo, "Build Your Social Resilience," para. 4.
12. Exod 4:10 (NRSV).

incident or when we face challenges that are private, the onus is on us to reach out to others. In the hospice and bereavement work that I did as a chaplain, I would often hear how lonely it felt for the survivors several months, even years, after their loved ones' deaths. Other family members had reengaged their lives, and friends had all but forgotten. Meanwhile, the survivors were still working to manage the waves of grief and despair singlehandedly. Perhaps we feel like we should not *have* to reach out. We think, "Don't they care? Why don't they call?" But realistically, the individuals who serve as our personal connections often do *not* know our needs unless we take the risk to articulate them, which can be intimidating and uncomfortable. When we ask for support or help, we will likely receive it. Even Jesus relied on companionship throughout his life. In the Garden of Gethsemane, he asked for support in his grief prior to his crucifixion. Jesus said to his closest friends, "I am deeply grieved, even to death; remain here, and stay awake with me."[13] Having strong connections with others is a key element of resilience.

CONNECTIONS WITH COMMUNITIES

In addition to individuals, we can find a sense of social connection in community. Communities can take a wide variety of forms and can serve essential purposes for our well-being and resilience. A London pastor said this almost two hundred years ago:

> Ye cannot live for yourselves; a thousand fibres connect you with your fellow-men, and along those fibres, as along sympathetic threads, run your actions as causes, and return to you as effects. Ye sin not for yourselves; ye cannot sin for yourselves; ye are members of a body, and as no member can suffer alone, neither can any be injurious alone.[14]

We are all connected to one another, and we do not suffer alone. There are many different communities in which we can find strength and support. These groups can be big or small, virtual or real, and religious or secular, and they may focus around activism, advocacy, or mutual support. Examples include the Moral Monday Movement, Alcoholics Anonymous, religious orders for Catholic sisters and brothers, the #MeToo movement,

---

13. Matt 26:38 (NRSV).
14. Melvill, "Partaking," 2:454.

Mothers Against Drunk Driving, and also the small communities we might discover in a church small group, support group, Arabic class, soccer team, or neighborhood. These communities can give us a sense of belonging, purpose, connection, support, and worth.

One community that helped me endure repeated grief and loss were my professional colleagues on my hospice team at our inpatient hospice facility in Massachusetts. I served as the chaplain and was responsible for providing spiritual and emotional support to patients, families, and staff in the acute care facility. It was a challenging place to work because end-of-life care is emotionally fraught and the patients who came to the facility were often young parents, children, or someone's life-long partner. Every staff member, including me, was guilty of growing to love our patients and their families. We were extremely close knit, and we kept each other's spirits up through encouragement, listening, and sometimes humor.

One winter day, I was at a patient's bedside. He was calm and unresponsive, approaching the end of his life. The medical staff and I had been in and out to check on him and his family throughout the day. At one point, I was sitting with him, cradling his hand when the nurse manager Dianne knocked quietly and entered the room. She leaned down and quietly, but sternly and unexpectedly, said, "I need to see you in the garage." The garage was a cold, cinderblock, unwelcoming space in the lower level where the hearses would come to pick up the deceased, not a place for a meeting. Curious, I made my way down to the garage and found the staff assembled there. In their midst was a colorful piñata dangling from the rafters. Dianne had planned a short celebration for a staff member's birthday, and we took turns being blindfolded and swinging at the piñata. When the candy came bursting forth, I dove on the floor, scooping up candy maniacally with my outstretched arms, with tears of both grief and laughter pouring from my eyes. Through our shared experiences, we could appreciate the contrast of the intensity our ministries with the ridiculousness of that piñata. We returned with plenty of time to say our final goodbyes to our patient, with our hearts open wider and with our spirits renewed. I will never forget the comfort that unexpected respite brought, the love that we all shared in that zany moment, and those dear colleagues who helped me do that incredibly rich and challenging ministry. Being a part of a community can be a lifesaver.

Sometimes we can find personal connections in virtual communities. Social media can be toxic; however, I was comforted by the "me too" community that was started by the activist Tarana Burke. Nearly two decades ago, a thirteen-year-old girl trusted Ms. Burke with her story of sexual abuse and suffering. That conversation inspired Ms. Burke to create a non-profit called Just Be Inc. because she recognized the importance of providing survivors of abuse with a community of support and resources.[15] In the spirit of solidarity and community, the hashtag #MeToo was recently shared on Facebook by millions of women who survived to sexual harassment and assault.[16] Finding support and encouragement from the "Silence Breakers" has empowered many and has reminded survivors of our worth, in spite of the ways that we may have felt bullied and silenced during our lives. It gave voice to the incidents many of us opted not to report and the feelings that we had buried. This movement is a community of support and encouragement, helping us realize that we are not alone. When some have been inclined to minimize or mock my experience, I am grateful for those in this virtual community who listen, believe, and understand.

For many religious and spiritual traditions, community is a central tenant. In Islam, for instance, there is an Arabic word "ummah," which can be translated as "community." One writer highlights that people in the Muslim community celebrate this principle "both religiously and emotionally," and she describes the broader Muslim community as a "frontierless brotherhood of men and women."[17] In Judaism, too, community is essential. The Hebrew Bible says, "How very good and pleasant it is when kindred live together in unity."[18] Similarly, the Christian New Testament includes a letter from the apostle Paul to the church in Corinth which describes us as all part of one body. He wrote, "God has so arranged the body, giving the greater honor to the inferior member, that there may be no dissension within the body, but the members may have the same care for one another. If one member suffers, all suffer together with it; if one member is honored, all rejoice together with it."[19] Likewise in Buddhism, community is important. The sangha can be translated as "community," and generally refers to the community of monastics. One writer says, "Taking refuge in the sangha means we find safety and strength in the fellow walkers of the path."[20] That quote is relevant to community more generally: in these varied communi-

---

15. Garcia, "Woman Who Created," paras. 1–4.

16. Khomami, "#MeToo," para. 6.

17. Rehmani, "Debating," 8.

18. Ps 133:1 (NRSV).

19. 1 Cor 12:24–26 (NRSV).

20. Sockolov, "Importance of Sangha," para. 2.

ties in which we find ourselves, we *can* discover "safety and strength with the fellow walkers of the path," whatever paths we may take.

BONDS WITH MENTORS AND MENTEES

In addition to individual relationships and community affiliations, social connections can be strengthened through mentorship. We benefit considerably when we go beyond superficial "networking" relationships and work to develop meaningful professional mentoring relationships that are rooted in trust and transparency with professional coaches or mentors. Successful people such as Sheryl Sandberg tout the benefits of having a professional ally who can provide us with insight, reassurance, and advice when we are struggling professionally.[21] In an article related to juvenile justice, a retired judge argues that mentors are also playing an essential role in helping reduce recidivism and estimates that there are over five thousand organizations in the United States dedicated to mentoring for youth.[22] Finding a mentor can help us be more resilient because they prove that obstacles can be overcome, they help illustrate a path of possibility, and they can provide wisdom and encouragement.

Our resilience is strengthened by having relationships with mentors, just as it is strengthened when *we* are the ones serving *others* in that way. Mentees are people that see *us* as mentors. When we are struggling, having people looking up to us is almost as important as having people we look up to. Knowing that my chaplain interns from Yale Divinity School were counting on me to be responsible, responsive, and calm helped me behave that way, even when I am feeling exhausted or frustrated. Mentees can bring out the best in us and help us see our skills, gifts, and strengths that we are tempted to minimize or deny. Mentees also help us see how far we have come and what we have achieved because they are often a few steps behind on the journey that we've taken. We do not need to be perfect to be a good mentor. Each of us has experience, gifts, and wisdom that could benefit others. Being a mentor helps us stay focused, inspires us to sharpen our skills, and does not allow us to become beholden to despair or burnout. We can look for ways to become mentors, perhaps through our faith communities, organizations such as Big Brothers Big Sisters, foster

21. Sandberg, "Sheryl Sandberg," 2:28.
22. Edwards, "Mentors Crucial," para. 2.

parenting, or within our professional settings. We have more to offer than we might think!

IDENTIFYING ROLE MODELS

In studies of both adults and children, scholars identified that resilient people also had role models that helped enable them to face difficult situations.[23] As a hospice chaplain, I met a frail, middle-aged woman from the Jewish tradition who was very near the end of her life. She remained quite lucid and alert, and after several visits, she shared with me a vision she was having—she kept seeing her deceased grandmother standing ominously at the foot of her bed. Although seeing images of deceased loved ones while one's death approaches was something I heard about often in my hospice work, this situation was unique. She said that her grandmother was the *last* person she wanted to see. This vision was not comforting in the *least* because her grandmother had been surly and stern. But as this patient reflected more deeply on this person's life, she acknowledged that Grandma had apparently been nearly blind and dauntlessly raised her ten children independently throughout the depression. The patient realized the meaning of this visit, saying, "She wasn't kind, but she was the strongest person I have ever known. She is here to remind me of my inner strength right now. She is telling me that I can face these last weeks with courage." Several weeks later, my patient died peacefully with the unexpected help of her austere grandma, for whom she was deeply grateful.

We can find role models to embolden our resilience in a variety of settings. They can be true or fictional, alive or deceased, and they need not be perfect. I have found many sources of inspiration in Christian writings such as in the faithfulness of Jesus's mother Mary, the boldness of the hemorrhaging woman who touched Jesus's cloak for healing, the wisdom of Esther, the perseverance of Paul, and the deep love and commitment of Mary Magdalene. Many followers of Islam look to the life of Muhammad, peace be upon him, for inspiration and guidance, and they deeply value the hadith, writings that describe his life, priorities, practices, and choices. Whether we are inspired by a specific guru, family member, deity, politician, or author, identifying and celebrating role models will increase our resilience.

23. Southwick and Charney, *Resilience*, 115.

"SO GRATEFUL FOR THIS TRIBE"

My dear friend Erica greets everyone she meets with her bubbly personality, incredible warmth, and generous empathy, and she has found strength throughout her life in the personal connections she has developed and nurtured. She is the person who is genuinely eager to befriend her Uber drivers, admirals, professors, wayfarers, custodians, politicians, baristas, and colleagues. Perhaps what truly represents her life and relationships is her curious hobby of making human pyramids, similar to how cheerleaders might form a human triangle by kneeling on one another in tiers. Her social media feed is full of her pyramids that include hikers, military officers, athletes, friends, strangers, and family members from around the world. These pyramids are a visual illustration of her commitment to social connection and the high value she places on relationships with others.

When you look at her life and biography, it is full of remarkable accomplishments and awards. She served twenty years as a commissioned officer in the U.S. Coast Guard before her retirement, and she is currently the executive director of an international nonprofit dedicated to empowering women and girls in Tanzania. In her spare time, she has been committed to the redevelopment of her community, hiked on Mounts Kilimanjaro and Everest, sponsored a number of children through Children International, and raised tens of thousands of dollars for a non-profit that helps families in Africa. Erica is beloved by many, shown by her service as a bridesmaid in fourteen weddings and the overflowing attendances at her recent birthday party and retirement ceremony. Her connections are so strong that when she traveled around the world for three months, there were only four nights that she stayed in a hotel instead of enjoying the comfort of a warm guest bed or couch of a friend. Unlike anyone else I know, Erica has a deep passion for making and maintaining social connections, and she is an amazing role model for how to develop and nurture individual connections, build connections with communities all over the world, create important mentoring connections, and look to role models for guidance and inspiration.

Erica and I have been friends since our basic training program at the Coast Guard Academy twenty-five years ago. The transition from civilian life to the academy was extremely challenging for all of us, and we quickly came to realize how desperately we needed one another. The hazing and harassment were relentless, which were made worse by the stresses of being away from home for the first time, living into a new and unknown vocation, and the constant struggle to find our inner and physical strength to endure.

Only days after the dehumanizing haircut, our introduction to morning calisthenics, and the beginning of our indoctrination, we were required to complete the dreaded Physical Fitness Exam. This exam involved a variety of elements, including a timed mile and a half run, which was apparently *not* one of Erica's strengths. She was fretful and exhausted, feeling hopeless as she was anxiously preparing for the 13.5 laps around the indoor track in the impossibly humid and intimidating gym, second-guessing herself and her choice to be a cadet. Erica's platoon leader, Ms. O'Brien, only knew Erica for a few days but quietly diagnosed Erica's despair. Counter to the culture, Ms. O'Brien gave Erica the extra encouragement that she desperately needed. An incredibly gifted athlete, this platoon leader ran every step of that race at Erica's side, helping Erica set a pace that would enable her to pass. That moment has inspired Erica to do the same for many others, reaching out a hand, helping someone keep pace, providing encouragement and positivity, and showing compassion and love.

Erica graduated four years later with high marks and many friends. She credits the community of amazing classmates, leaders, and roommates that helped her survive the ups and downs of life at a military academy. She felt ready for her next substantial life change. Erica left Connecticut in the summer of 1996 to report to her first unit, a 180-foot seagoing buoy tender whose homeport was in the beautiful Pacific Northwest. After many months of navigation training, ship-driving exercises, and hands-on drills, Erica became qualified as a deck watch officer, serving as one of the people responsible for the navigation and safety of the ship while underway. Although she trained for many different scenarios, she could never have predicted what would happen just a few months later.

It was late in the evening when Erica assumed the watch. The ship had just finished its maintenance work on a buoy, and it was time for the ship to head up the river toward its homeport. It was a calm evening, but the fog was incredibly thick, making the ship dependent on its radar to monitor its position and local ship traffic. Erica and her navigation team identified an enormous container ship maneuvering outbound in the same river. The ships discussed the time and location that they would pass one another in the channel, but the timing of the passing of the vessels could not have been worse. The ships would pass one another at a sharp turn in the channel, and as the container ship emerged from the fog, a collision seemed imminent. Erica ordered the sounding of the danger signal of five short blasts and made evasive maneuvers to try to avoid the collision. As the crew braced for impact, they were thinking of the twenty-three sailors who died in a collision a decade earlier on an identical vessel.

Although Erica navigated her ship far outside the channel to give the larger container ship plenty of room, the pilot of the container ship did not adequately account for the tide and swung too wide when making the turn. The experience was like pulling over to the shoulder on your side of the road, only to be hit by the eighteen-wheeler coming from the opposite direction. The bow of the container ship smashed against the port bridge wing of the buoy tender and devastated it, throwing Erica's ship out of control and her captain to the ground.[24] Thankfully, the injuries were minimal, and the ship was able to be repaired and remain in service. Although it was determined that Erica was not to blame, few Coast Guard careers survive the shame and trauma of a collision at sea. She was heartbroken at the possibility of being released from active duty, in shame over her sense of responsibility for the captain's injuries and the peril of the crew, and now insecure about her abilities as a ship-driver and Coast Guard officer. Erica was certain that she would be a scapegoat, destined to live with this albatross forever. Just as she was processing these complex feelings soon after the incident, the crewmembers presented her with a surprise. The sailors gave her two dozen white roses with a note reading, "We will sail with you anywhere," and bearing the signatures of the crew.

To this day, Erica has kept and cherished that note of support and encouragement. Her service survived that terrifying day, and she has been an incredible officer and mentor to many since. Years later, she found herself at the place where her Coast Guard career began, at the academy. There, she was responsible for leadership development and saw a substantial need for extra support, networking, and mentoring for young women officers who sometimes find themselves in hostile workplaces, with little confidence or experience, and with little power. She was instrumental in creating the Women's Leadership Initiative, a national movement focused on increasing retention of women in the Coast Guard through policy change, mentorship, and professional development. She has become a mentor to many successful and high-achieving women, and she has found that these relationships have helped sustain *her* and have provided her a sense of purpose and meaning. It was during this chapter of her life that she experienced another unexpected challenge.

24. "Marine Accident Brief," 6–9.

Erica is incredible about staying connected with our academy class-mates and even coordinated a monthly gathering for classmates living in Connecticut. We chatted and visited periodically, but it was a surprise to see an incoming call from Erica while I was chasing my two kids at the lake one hot summer day. She told me she was in a Waterbury hospital with her family at her father's bedside. He was unexpectedly hospitalized from complications from his chronic condition, and he had very little time left. She knew I was trained as a hospital chaplain and asked me to come. When I arrived, he had just died. His wife, sister, daughters, son, and son-in-law were at the bedside. I joined them at his bedside, learning more about his amazing life and contribution, supporting the family, and offering prayer. As the days and weeks passed, many other members of Erica's support sys-tem came to provide her support. At the funeral, the small country church was overflowing with loving people, and her family grew even closer to one another. Erica and her family were grief-stricken, but they were able to endure the pain with the help of their community of love that came out to support them.

Doubtlessly, Erica was transformed by these extraordinarily chal-lenging events in her life in large part because of the help of others. She recognizes and values the ways that people have supported her through her difficulties, and she finds deep purpose in providing similar comfort and assistance to others. Her story illustrates the important roles of individuals, communities, mentors, mentees, and role models.

FINAL THOUGHTS ON PEOPLE

Whether our social connections are related to individuals, communities, mentors, mentees, or role models, I think it would be fun if we could em-brace our thirteen-year-old selves and have posters of our sources of inspi-ration tacked up to our bedroom walls. I was a catcher on my high school softball team, and I went to bed every night looking at my favorite poster of a smiling Gary Carter from the New York Mets hanging on my closet door. His work ethic, talent, moral aptitude, and likability deeply inspired me (okay, I also loved his beautifully permed hair!). Fast-forward to today: if you were to visit my office at the university, you would see pictures of my husband and kids, my sister and parents, two encouraging and caring college students I met during my first bumpy year as the university chap-lain, my childhood pastor, Rosie the Riveter, Jesus's mother Mary, women suffragists, Jesus, and Norman Rockwell's *Girl with Black Eye*. Okay, I admit that Bill Clinton is there too (like I said, perfection is not a requirement!). All these people have been deeply inspiring to me, and I am moved and encouraged every time I look up to see their kind and loving faces looking back at me and am reminded of their strength, endurance, grit, and wisdom. Who are those people for you? Let's surround ourselves with their messages, images, inspiration, or wisdom. Developing meaningful relationships with individuals, communities, mentors, and mentees will provide us with support and love, a sense of connection and belonging, and wisdom and guidance. Identifying and celebrating role models, flawed as they may be, will inspire our choices and help improve our outlook. Evidence shows that social connection is the strongest predictor of how long we will live,[25] so developing personal connections will doubtlessly help us become more resilient, and you might be surprised at how much fun you have doing it!

REFLECTION AND ACTION

Questions to ponder

- With whom in your life can you share anything at all, and you know they will continue to love you unconditionally?

- What are your fears related to being honest and transparent with others? What barriers exist between you and those closest to you? What are their roots?

- If you have a pet, how is your relationship with her or him?

- Consider your relationship with a spiritual leader, therapist, spiritual director, pastoral counselor, or psychiatrist whom you would call if there were a crisis in your life. How have they been helpful to you? If you cannot identify any person, what steps might you take to create such a relationship?

- To which clubs, communities, and organizations do you belong that are uplifting and life giving? What do you love about them? If you are not associated with any, with which clubs, communities, or organizations might you consider connecting?

---

25. Pinker, "Secret to Living."

- In which spiritual communities do you feel at home, and how often do you affiliate with them? Can you describe a time that a spiritual community has provided you with something you needed spiritually or emotionally?

- Who inspires you? How do they inspire you?

- Are there people who are deceased whose lives you find inspirational? What have they done that you find meaningful or impressive? What gifts and skills did they employ? What did they have to overcome to do it?

- Who looks to you as a teacher or mentor, and how often do you meet with them? What gifts do you have that you share with them?

Strategies for cultivating this characteristic of resilience

- Identify barriers that exist between you and people who are close to you and work to remove or reduce some of those barriers.

- Write in your journal about the person who most positively affected you that day and how.

- Write a thank-you note (for no specific reason) to someone who has had a positive impact on your life and describe what you appreciate about the individual and what he or she has done for you.

- Send holiday cards to people who have had a positive impact on your life.

- Make it a habit to write or email thank-you notes to people who support you or do something kind for you, particularly your mentors.

- Establish concrete goals about the frequency with which you will reach out to mentors, mentees, and confidants, both electronically and in person. Invite them for lunch, a walk, coffee, or other activity.

- Consider the feasibility of adopting a pet for support and companionship, if that seems comforting to you.

- Commit to finding a spiritual and/or religious community that is comfortable and safe for you. Even if you don't identify as "religious," there are many diverse spiritual communities that might be a great fit. I acknowledge that this can be an emotionally draining task, but it can be so worthwhile! Ask about opportunities to connect with a small group, and get involved with their extracurricular programing or volunteer opportunities.

- Be intentional about cultivating community in the clubs and organizations with which you are connected, such as hosting a potluck social for the soccer team, having lunch with colleagues, or hosting dinner parties or gatherings for friends or neighbors.

- Seek to connect with people or groups with whom you share a hobby or interest such as photography, mountain biking, or knitting.

- Identify people—alive or deceased—that have been inspirational to you. Discern how you can learn more about their lives and consider how you can celebrate and remember them.

Prayer

Spirit of Love, your grace-filled spirit connects all living things. Help us to embrace our imperfections and risk being transparent. Help us to love ourselves, laugh at ourselves, and be gentle with ourselves, appreciating that we are blessed and beautiful just as we are. Help us to identify supporting and loving people in our lives and give us the courage and wisdom to reach out to them when we need help and encouragement. Please help protect us from toxic people and situations and insulate those we love from meanness and hate. Guide us toward communities that are life-giving and affirming and beautiful, where we can be ourselves and be upheld for the work and service to which we are called. Thank you for the mentors in our lives who have inspired us and guided us, and in gratitude, enable us to be helpful and loving mentors to others, trusting that we do not need to be perfect but only need hearts of helpfulness and love. Spirit of Hope, when we feel despair or despondency, help us to recognize role models who can provide us with inspiration and hope and help us to feel supported by a great cloud of witnesses who have gone before us. We specifically offer our thanks for these special and inspirational people and communities who have been essential to our survival and joy: (list names here). Amen.

2

Positivity

Let's rise and be thankful,
for if we didn't learn a lot today, at least we may have learned a little.
And if we didn't learn even a little, at least we didn't get sick.
And if we did get sick, at least we didn't die. So let us all be thankful.

—BUDDHIST TEACHER QUOTED BY LEO BUSCAGLIA[1]

POSITIVITY IS THE INTENTION to focus on the things in our lives that are
going well, to notice the benefit and blessings in our circumstances, and
to celebrate the relationships, events, and achievements that give us joy.
Positivity is a proven characteristic of resilience that has been explored by
scholars as long ago as Plato and Aristotle.[2] Our collective curiosity about
positivity has never abated. Norman Vincent Peale's *The Power of Positive
Thinking* held a spot on the *New York Times* bestseller list for 186 weeks,
and it has been one of the best-selling spiritual books of all time behind
the Bible.[3] Self-help books related to happiness and positivity are abundant,
and the positive psychology course at Harvard recently set a record for the
most popular class in the history of the university.[4] On some level, many

1. Unnamed Buddhist teacher, quoted in Buscaglia, *Born for Love*, 102.
2. Grenville-Cleave, *Positive Psychology*, 1.
3. Vecsey, "Norman Vincent Peale," para. 33.
4. Pennock, "Positive Psychology 1504," para. 1.

of us acknowledge the relationship between positivity and resilience and recognize our power to cultivate this important habit.

Positivity *is* a habit. Habits are behaviors and responses that we practice and engrain in our minds by doing them consistently, intentionally or not. Habits dictate 40 to 95 percent of our actions,[5] including our mindless commutes to work, the subconscious rolling of our eyes when we are frustrated, and the warm-hearted or unfriendly thoughts that pop into our minds. This Zen tale illustrates this:

> Out of nowhere, a horse came galloping hurriedly down the road with a man in the saddle, holding on desperately. Another man standing alongside the road thought he must be in a rush to be somewhere and yelled, "Where are you going?" The man in the saddle responded, "I don't know! Ask the horse!"[6]

This galloping horse symbolizes our "habit energy" that drives us in a certain direction because of ways we have done things in the past.[7] This story invites us to more mindfully control the direction of our "horses" by creating new, healthy, intentional habits such as embracing positivity.

Many of us justifiably cringe when we hear someone enthusiastically chirp, "Just look at the bright side!" or "Think positive!" but positivity is a habit we *can* cultivate, and it has played an important role throughout the history of many religious and spiritual traditions. The book of Proverbs in the Hebrew Bible says, "A cheerful heart is a good medicine, but a downcast spirit dries up the bones."[8] Rumi, a Muslim poet and theologian from the thirteenth century, encouraged a tolerance and reframing of negativity by rhetorically asking, "If you are irritated by every rub, how will your mirror be polished?"[9] The Christian Bible also addresses positivity in this quote from the apostle Paul:

> Whatever is true, whatever is honorable, whatever is just, whatever is pure, whatever is pleasing, whatever is commendable, if there is any excellence and if there is anything worthy of praise, think about these things.[10]

---

5. Walesh, "Using the Power," para. 2.

6. Original source unknown.

7. Valentine, "6 Awesome Zen Stories," § 5.

8. Prov 17:22 (NRSV).

9. Rumi, quoted in Adams Helminski, *Rumi Daylight*, 69.

10. Phil 4:8 (NRSV).

Positive thinking is consistently encouraged.

Buddhism generally looks at positive thinking in a slightly different way. While burying or suppressing negative feelings can be seen as inauthentic, some who follow Buddhism engage in positive thinking based on their belief that perceiving situations and events with feelings of calmness and compassion can help us relate to experiences with more healthy perspectives and ultimately transform those situations in helpful ways.[11] In other words, like many religious and spiritual traditions, Buddhism appreciates that our experiences are largely influenced by how we perceive them. The Buddha was quoted as saying the following: "All that we are is the result of what we have thought: it is founded on our thoughts, it is made up of our thoughts. If a man speaks or acts with a pure thought, happiness follows him, like a shadow that never leaves him."[12]

Thich Nhat Hanh is a Vietnamese Zen Buddhist monk, teacher, writer, and activist who established an organization in Vietnam that helped people rebuild their homes and neighborhoods and established hospitals and schools.[13] He continues to work tirelessly traveling, teaching, mentoring, and advocating for peace. Amid this busyness, he is famous for his calm, peaceful, mindful spirit. He believes that we each have different seeds within our consciousness, and the seeds we water are the seeds that flourish. He said the following:

> A good practitioner knows how to keep the negative seeds here (in the storehouse consciousness), and tries by his or her practice to help the positive seeds to manifest. If the positive seeds continue to manifest here, the negative seeds become smaller, smaller, less important. When they are tiny, not important, it is difficult for them to manifest.[14]

He invites us to water the seeds of positivity so we can live more freely and peacefully. We can water these seeds of positivity by focusing on the positive when we think of ourselves and others and by embracing the positive as we reflect on our past, present, and future circumstances. Sometimes, though, doing that is challenging, so let's first acknowledge what might get in the way of practicing positivity.

11. Burk, "Changing Reality," para. 4.

12. Buddha, quoted in Burk, "Changing Reality," para. 10.

13. *New World Encyclopedia*, s.v. "Thich Nhat Hanh," http://www.newworldencyclopedia.org/entry/Thich_Nhat_Hanh.

14. Nhat Hanh, "Watering," para. 50.

BARRIERS TO POSITIVITY

As many of us know from personal experience, there are barriers that can interfere with our ability to adopt a more positive outlook. First, we tend to weigh negative comments more heavily than positive ones.[15] Over a decade ago, I delivered a sermon one Sunday at my home church. I received a variety of comments from the kind-hearted congregation that knew me well. Guess which comment I remember today, many years later—the one critical comment from a man who pointed out that my sermon illustration about the pioneering Wright brothers had a minor factual inaccuracy. I am not alone; we apparently need approximately three times more positive emotions to balance out negative emotions.[16] Although the specificity of this ratio has been debated, the fact that we need more positive events, emotions, and experiences to outweigh the negative appears undeniable.

We are also inclined to compare ourselves to others, especially in the age of social media. I see my friend's Facebook photos of her beautiful and creative lunches that she makes for her sons and wonder why I'm barely able to slap together a peanut butter and jelly sandwich on a frozen hotdog bun (the only bread I sometimes have in stock) before frantically running them to school as the late bell is ringing. Having a positive attitude about life is more difficult when everyone else seems to be going on fabulous vacations, celebrating anniversaries and birthdays with their perfect children and partners, and enjoying relaxing nights out at basketball games, museums, and restaurants. Frankly, taking a break from social media during Lent did wonders for my positivity!

Resisting the temptation to compare ourselves to others is essential, especially since the snippets of life revealed in social media and in magazines are often doctored and do not tell the full story. When I was visiting with friends recently in Washington, DC, one friend said to another, "I love following you on social media; your life is so fun and adventurous!" My friend wisely responded, "I only post the good stuff! Don't compare the best 5 percent of my life with 100 percent of yours!" Even *The Chronicle of Higher Education*, a publication for college faculty and administrators, warns about "imposter syndrome" and the insecurity that grows out of comparing ourselves to others.[17] We are unique individuals, and as won-

---

15. Grenville-Cleave, *Positive Psychology*, 16.

16. Research by Barbara Fredrickson and Marcial Losada, cited in ibid., 28.

17. Revuluri, "How to Overcome," para. 1.

derful as we may be, there will always be people that are smarter, more attractive, and funnier, and our resilience benefits when we choose not to compare ourselves with others.

We may also believe that having a positive attitude is inauthentic. Working to cultivate a positive attitude absolutely does *not* mean that we are not entitled to grieve, be frustrated, experience anger, or feel resentment. Those are natural and unavoidable feelings, and burying them in an effort to be more positive is unhealthy and unproductive. After returning home for break during my first semester at seminary, I vividly remember my parents sitting me down on the floral couch in the living room to tell me of the unexpected death of my beloved mentor, Reverend Cotter, our church pastor of eighteen years, from a heart attack. At "Rev's" memorial service, I was sitting and crying in the pew and was approached by a fellow congregant whom I knew well. She asked—earnestly and curiously, not sarcastically—"Since you're in seminary, I would think your faith is strong and you must be pretty confident that he's in a better place. I am surprised to see you crying so much." I explained that I was grieving his absence in my life. She seemed relieved to hear me say that. I was grieving while also celebrating the many gifts of wisdom he imparted on me and the precious hours he spent teaching and guiding me through his sermons, the youth group, and our outings for coffee at the diner. Feeling grief, acknowledging our pain, and giving voice to our hurt do *not* mean we are negative people, rather it shows our willingness to love deeply and be vulnerable. Grief and positivity are not mutually exclusive.

Sometimes, there are physiological conditions that affect our ability to be positive, such as clinical depression or clinical anxiety. Although positive thinking alone cannot cure depression or anxiety, one study showed that therapeutic interventions based on positive psychology were more satisfying to patients than interventions focused only on cogitative behavioral therapy.[18] Working to increase positive emotions can reduce symptoms of depression,[19] and positive thinking can play a helpful role in coping and in building resilience, even if we struggle with some baseline depression or anxiety.

Maintaining a positive attitude is like a marathon. It takes months, maybe years, of training, practice, and discipline to prepare. It is unlikely that a person could wake up one morning and run a marathon. Similarly,

18. Lopez et al., "Comparing the Acceptability," 1029.

19. Ackerman, "How Can Positive Psychology Help," para. 4.

we won't just wake up one day with a positive outlook on life. It is something we need to cultivate, nurture, and habitualize. Also, we are never officially "finished" with the work that is required. When preparing for a marathon, we can't quit training and expect to run a race a year later; consistent and sustained training is needed. Likewise, we need to practice positivity in the mundane circumstances on a daily basis so that having a positive outlook is a realistic possibility when we need it the most—when we are in our darkest valleys. We can begin this "training" by focusing on the positive when we think of ourselves and others and as we reflect on our past, present, and future circumstances.

POSITIVITY IN OUR VIEW OF OURSELVES

The first step in developing positivity is to understand our intrinsic value, importance, and capability—to learn to love ourselves. This has nothing to do with being perfect or not making mistakes. It does not mean that we are oblivious to the ways we can improve ourselves physically, emotionally, and spiritually through self-care, counseling, healthy lifestyle choices, and healthy relationships. Loving ourselves means genuinely appreciating ourselves and being patient with ourselves, understanding that we are forever on a journey toward increased wellness, wholeness, and joy.

Many of us struggle with issues related to self-esteem and self-worth. The popular author and researcher Brené Brown has been incredibly successful relating to people about issues of worthiness, shame, self-compassion, and vulnerability. Her popularity is not a surprise; 60 percent of women engage in negative thinking about themselves at least once a week and struggle with self-love.[20] In her book *Rising Strong*, Brown says, "Just because someone isn't willing or able to love us, it doesn't mean that we are unlovable."[21] When we shower ourselves with criticism, doubt, and even self-loathing, we limit ourselves. We prevent ourselves from trying something new or challenging. We refrain from setting ambitious goals for ourselves. Honestly, I was inspired to move forward on this resilience book project by a social media meme posted by a beloved and brilliant friend Courtney, which said, "There are people less qualified than you, doing the things you want to do, simply because they decided to believe in themselves." I was so busy doubting myself and feeling inadequate and

20. Capretto, "Brené Brown," para. 2.
21. Brown, *Rising Strong*, 82.

insecure that I was unwilling to take that first step. Low self-esteem can be disabling and life limiting, and we can work to improve our self-esteem by discovering our value in a spiritual sense, by embracing positive self-talk, by minimizing our self-blame, and by embracing our "growing edges" (I prefer this gentle term over "weaknesses" or "faults" to refer to the things about ourselves that could use some tweaking or upgrading).

Many spiritual and religious frameworks celebrate the uniqueness and giftedness of each of us as individuals. For those who believe in a higher power or divine creator, it may be comforting to remember that God created us in God's image, and God did not mess up when God made us. Those in the Abrahamic traditions are encouraged by our holy writings to love ourselves and appreciate our gifts. The Psalms state: "I praise you, for I am fearfully and wonderfully made. Wonderful are your works; that I know very well."[22] In the Buddhist tradition, people may seek contentment and endeavor to practice "non-attachment." This concept helps them release expectations and cravings and work toward happiness. During meditation, there is often a gentle redirection for those of us unable to maintain focus, not a self-destructive, judging admonishment. The concept of being gentle with ourselves is an important aspect of building our self-esteem.

How we talk to ourselves influences our self-esteem. Positive self-talk improves our self-esteem, just as negative self-talk diminishes our self-esteem. When I lead workshops about resilience, I sometimes offer an exercise related to negative thinking and invite people to write down on a small sheet of paper the negative thing that they say to themselves most often.[23] A co-facilitator and I then read those messages to one another using "you" in the mean voices that likely go along with these terrible statements. "You are fat, and nobody will ever love you." "You are an imposter and everyone knows that you don't know what you're talking about at work." "People find you annoying." It relentlessly goes on and on. The purpose is to help people see the ugliness and destructiveness of this language they use against themselves. Participants have said that it is hard for them to not stop us in the middle because it is so hard to hear such hateful things said to another, yet we do it to ourselves every day. I look around and see a circle filled with beautiful, loving, compassionate, intelligent, caring people, yet I am hearing destructive and hurtful phrases that are truly heartrending. At the conclusion, people share about what it was like to hear the self-judgments

---

22. Ps 139:14 (NRSV).

23. Workshop exercise was inspired by Iris, "Best Friends."

read aloud. We identify the many common themes that often arise, and then we go around the circle, saying something loving about ourselves and something positive about the person next to us. It is incredible to see the energy change as people affirm themselves and experience affirmation from their neighbors.

The negative comments we say to ourselves have many origins, but one source might be those things we have heard and internalized from others in our lives, such as judgmental parents or partners, critical teachers, and envious friends. When we hear nasty things said to us by people we are taught to trust and respect, it is nearly impossible to dismiss them easily. In a parenting article from *Psychology Today*, Melanie Greenberg says, "Kids internalize these negative labels and begin to see themselves as 'not good enough.' Humiliating or shaming a kid can shape brain pathways in negative ways."[24] For some of us, our brain pathways desperately need to be reshaped with affirmation, positivity, and love. We are complex, sensitive, and hopeful people, and negative self-talk truly limits our ability to take risks, achieve, and enjoy life.

In addition to avoiding negative self-talk, resisting the tendency to blame ourselves for our challenges and problems benefits our self-esteem. Certainly, we need to take responsibility for mistakes we make. Doing so enables us to learn, grow, and make necessary modifications to our behavior or interactions. On the other hand, excessive self-blame is damaging and can hinder our ability to have a positive attitude and can even lead to self-harm or suicide.[25] We may become stuck in a place of self-judgment—wondering why we ended up in that situation, how we could have prevented it, or what we wish we had done differently. We sometimes believe that our own character flaws and inadequacies are entirely to blame for our missteps or unfortunate choices. A negative self-image hampers our resilience and makes us question our ability to overcome obstacles, solve problems, and heal.

In the introduction to the book, I shared the story of my unsanctioned relationship that led to my resignation from military service and the deep shame, grief, and regret I felt. For many years after my resignation, I relentlessly replayed the words of my executive officer (similar to a vice principal, in some ways), who had initiated the punitive action against us. He looked me with a cold, severe expression, wagged his finger in my face, and said,

24. Greenberg, "Worst Mistakes," § 3.
25. Sreenivasan and Weinberger, "Self-Blame," para. 8.

"Don't blame anyone but yourself. This is all *your* fault." He did not need to tell me that; I was already an insecure twenty-three-year-old who was incredibly hard on myself, who internalized the shame, took full responsibility, and believed that I was fatally flawed and forever destined to fail. I left the service with fear and insecurity that haunted me for years.

After years of counseling, I recognize that I obviously could have managed situations significantly more creatively and fruitfully in the Coast Guard, but I can also see the many ways that the toxic aspects of the Coast Guard Academy culture and some expressly hostile shipmates at my unit contributed to the erosion of my self-esteem and played a critical role in this painful and life-changing event. Realizing this has empowered me to live more boldly and confidently, to be more aware of the importance of solving problems proactively, to take better care of myself emotionally and spiritually, and to trust my ability to make good choices. We will be more resilient if we make an effort to maintain a rational, objective view of our mistakes and setbacks and resist the temptation for excessive self-blame.

When we come to a place where we can see our imperfections and "growing edges" as endearing quirks, and we see our endeavors to improve as fun and healthy exercises, we become more resilient people. Theologian and Catholic priest Henri Nouwen's book entitled *The Wounded Healer* is an incredible testimony of how woundedness can enable us to be more compassionate. He said, "The great illusion of leadership is to think that [people] can be led out of the desert by someone who has never been there."[26] Often, our suffering and struggles uniquely equip us to be more emotionally responsive to others and invite us to be empowered by our experiences of overcoming difficulty as we face our current and future challenges. And once we adopt a positive view of ourselves, we are able to view others in a more positive way. Maya Angelou said, "I don't trust people who don't love themselves and tell me, 'I love you.' There is an African saying which is: 'Be careful when a naked person offers you a shirt.'"[27]

POSITIVITY IN OUR VIEW OF OTHERS

Another part of our developing a more positive attitude is working to view others more positively by cultivating empathy. One program that embraces the importance of empathy and loving others is the Ana Grace Project, an

26. Nouwen, *Wounded Healer*, 72.

27. Angelou, "Distinguished Annie Clark Tanner Lecture."

initiative named for a vibrant little girl who was among the children shot and killed in the Newtown school massacre. This organization was created by her loving family and focuses attention on creating healthy communities through encouraging relationships with others, empathy, self-care and play, service to others, and respect for others.[28] This incredible non-profit invites people to "choose love" and believes that showing kindness and love toward others is the key to preventing violence and making our communities safer. "Choosing love" does not only benefit our communities, it benefits us as individuals and makes us more resilient. Loving others can be a challenge, but with practice—and prayer, perhaps—discovering empathy for others, even those who are undeserving, is a healthy choice, and love for others can be developed through the following: giving others the benefit of the doubt and being generous with our forgiveness.

Giving someone the benefit of the doubt is a form of grace. When someone is unkind to us, drives aggressively or disrespectfully, or even does us harm, it can be incredibly helpful if we resist assuming they had negative intentions and give them some unearned grace, even if they don't deserve it. I was the one about to give birth in the passenger seat of our Honda while my husband drove aggressively to the hospital's maternity center. Another time, I was the one whose unexpected health problem required much more time than the doctor allotted, blowing her appointment schedule and making many subsequent patients wait interminably in the office. I've been the one in the wrong lane who realized I needed to do a three-lane sweep to get off on the correct exit. So when I'm cut off or waiting forever in the doctor's office, I work hard to remember those days and internalize this quote from the nineteenth century: "Let us not attribute to malice and cruelty what may be referred to less criminal motives. Do we not often afflict others undesignedly, and, from mere carelessness, neglect to relieve distress?"[29] It is likely that we have each inadvertently cut someone off, mindlessly stepped in front of someone in line without realizing, or forgotten to follow through on something important. I am so grateful when people simply wave instead of honk or when they politely explain that they had been waiting before I showed up. At times we are a victim, and at other times an aggressor, intentionally or not.

28. Ana Grace Project, anagraceproject.org.
29. West, *Loyalists*, 3:132.

Treating others the way we want to be treated is a key to embracing positivity in our view of others and is fundamental to nearly every religious tradition. The language of a few are detailed here:[30]

- Christianity: "Do unto others as you would have them do unto you."

- Confucianism: "One word which sums up the basis of all good conduct—lovingkindness. Do not do to others what you do not want done to yourself."

- Buddhism: "Hurt not others in ways that you yourself would find hurtful."

- Islam: "No one of you is a believer until he desires for his brother that which he desires for himself."

- Hinduism: "Do not to others what ye do not wish done to yourself; and wish for others too what ye desire and long for, for yourself."

- Judaism: "Love thy neighbor as thyself."

Giving other people grace with a spirit of love will make us more resilient people by helping us more fully embrace positivity in our view of others.

There are times, however, when people probably do not deserve the benefit of the doubt, and in those cases, forgiveness is called for. Forgiveness is an important part of embracing a more positive spirit because it prevents us from being contaminated by unresolved hurt and resentment. We often think of forgiveness as a discrete *response* that results from a conciliatory gesture such as an apology, but a better definition says it is "the act of pardoning an offender; ceasing to feel resentment toward him because of his offense and giving up all claim to recompense."[31] Brené Brown says, "Forgiveness is not forgetting or walking away from accountability or condoning a hurtful act; it's the process of taking back and healing our lives so we can truly live."[32] Forgiveness is a liberating *choice* to release the feelings of resentment and hurt.

Providing forgiveness *doesn't* mean we're not going to experience anger; anger can be healthy, appropriate, and unavoidable at times. Forgiveness *doesn't* mean we will reopen ourselves to mistreatment or abuse, tolerate any behavior that harms us, or stay with an abusive or neglectful

30. *Golden Rule* (poster).

31. *Watchtower Online Library*, s.v. "Forgiveness," https://wol.jw.org/en/wol/d/r1/lp-e/1200001554.

32. Brown, *Rising Strong*, 152.

partner. Forgiveness *doesn't* mean that we forget. The Christian ethicist and theologian Lewis Smedes said this:

> Forgiving does not erase the bitter past. A healed memory is not a deleted memory. Instead, forgiving what we cannot forget creates a new way to remember. We change the memory of our past into a hope for our future.[33]

Even with hopeful intentions, forgiveness *doesn't* happen overnight; it sometimes takes a lot of time, and it is rarely a one-time deal. We often need to revisit our forgiveness and recommit to it. As we choose to *practice* forgiveness, our resentments will subside with time, and as we *practice* forgiveness, it will come more naturally, both with healing our past hurts and with managing future offenses against us. The Baptist minister and civil rights activist Reverend Martin Luther King Jr. said,

> He who is devoid of the power to forgive is devoid of the power to love. It is impossible even to begin the act of loving one's enemies without prior acceptance of the necessity, over and over again, of forgiving those who inflict evil and injury upon us.[34]

Forgiveness is a key to positivity and will help us become more resilient. It is hard to be positive with the toxic anger and unresolved betrayal weighing on our hearts. Some might find inspiration from the words of Jesus. In the Christian Gospel of Matthew, one of Jesus's followers asked him, "Lord, how many times shall I forgive my brother or sister who sins against me? Up to seven times?" Jesus replied, "I tell you, not seven times, but seventy-seven times."[35] Jesus's actions on the cross were almost unfathomable and can also serve as an inspiration. Christian author Phillip Yancy explains it this way:

> In one of his last acts before death, Jesus forgave a thief dangling on a cross, knowing full well the thief had converted out of plain fear. That thief would never study the Bible, never attend synagogue or church, and never make amends to all those he had wronged. He simply said "Jesus, remember me," and Jesus promised, "Today you will be with me in paradise."[36]

---

33. Smedes, *Art of Forgiving*, 171.
34. King, "Loving Your Enemies."
35. Matt 18:21–22 (NIV).
36. Yancey, *What's So Amazing*, 54–55.

This generosity of spirit serves as a model for how we are called to treat others, even when it is difficult.

Ultimately, without a spirit that seeks to forgive, *we* suffer because we are "sticking it to ourselves." I think of an old Sprint PCS commercial in which a high-power executive is speaking with an employee and says, "With Sprint's new calling plan, no one can tell me what to do. I can talk when and how I want. It's my little way of sticking it to the man." His employee points out, "But you *are* the man, so I guess you're sticking it to yourself."[37] Similar in spirit, the following Zen tale about two monks speaks of our inclination to hold onto resentment, which ultimately has a negative effect on us:

> Tanzan and Ekido were once traveling together down a muddy road. A heavy rain was still falling. Coming around a bend, they met a lovely girl in a silk kimono and sash, unable to cross the intersection. "Come on, girl," said Tanzan at once. Lifting her in his arms, he carried her over the mud. Ekido did not speak again until that night when they reached a lodging temple. Then he no longer could restrain himself. "We monks don't go near females," he told Tanzan, "especially not young and lovely ones. It is dangerous. Why did you do that?" "I left the girl there," said Tanzan. "Are you still carrying her?"[38]

We have the opportunity to put down those burdens of anger and resentment that we carry and liberate ourselves from those who have already claimed too much of our joy.

We can avoid "sticking it to ourselves" by intentionally giving others the benefit of the doubt and being generous with our forgiveness. These practices can become habits that will enable us to more fully embrace positivity and become healthier, more full of love, and more resilient. Fred Rogers, an ordained pastor and beloved host of the TV show *Mister Rogers' Neighborhood*, said this in a college graduation address: "I believe that appreciation is a holy thing, that when we look for what's best in the person we happen to be with at the moment, we're doing what God does. So, in loving and appreciating our neighbor, we're participating in something truly sacred."[39] Working toward having a more positive view of ourselves and others will benefit our resilience and will enable us to more easily cultivate a more positive outlook on our past, present, and future circumstances.

37. Sprint, "Stickin' It to the Man."
38. Mujū, *101 Zen Stories*, no. 14.
39. Rogers, "Address."

POSITIVITY IN OUR VIEW OF PAST CIRCUMSTANCES

Focusing on positive memories helps us become more positive people. Ebenezer Scrooge's visit from the Ghost of Christmas Past in Charles Dickens's book *A Christmas Carol* is profound and revealing. The character's spirit lifts when he remembers the joy of playing with his dear childhood friends, the love of his caring younger sister, and the compassion and energy of his kindhearted and generous boss, Mr. Fezziwig. As the story unfolds, we learn that Scrooge's father was distant and apathetic, and his childhood was far from happy. Yet we see Scrooge become enlivened, even joy filled, as he recounts the *positive* memories. Recalling these happy memories empowered and inspired him. Like Scrooge, our life stories involve both positive and negative events and memories.

Unsurprisingly, research proves that "bad is stronger than good," and we are more likely to be affected by undesirable events, unkind people, and destructive emotions than we are by their positive counterparts because bad experiences have "longer lasting and more intense consequences" than good ones.[40] Whether we like it or not, there are mistakes we have made and betrayals we survived. There were likely chapters during which we felt misunderstood, alone, and marginalized. While these hurtful experiences are important parts of who we are and are absolutely worth processing in counseling or therapy, we *will* benefit if we make a concerted effort to recall and reminisce about positive memories. This helps us create a more positive view of our past and, ultimately, ourselves. This positivity will constructively infect our current mood and disposition, and it will beneficially affect how we view our current and future circumstances.

POSITIVITY IN OUR VIEW OF CURRENT CIRCUMSTANCES

Having a positive attitude about our current circumstances is an essential part of embracing positivity, even though it can be difficult. Martha Washington was born into privilege and married one of the greatest leaders of our nation, but like many of our own personal stories, Martha's story was riddled with sadness and setbacks. Two of Martha Washington's four children died in childhood. After being married seven years, her husband also died, leaving her a widow at the young age of twenty-five. She was fortunate to remarry, though, and she and President Washington raised the other

40. Baumeister et al., "Bad Is Stronger," 325.

two children. Her story then took another devastating twist—her surviving daughter died as a teenager during an epileptic seizure, and her last remaining child died from typhus contracted during military service soon after.[41] A woman whose life was so incredibly difficult—losing her first husband *and* all of her children—declared that happiness was a choice. She wrote this in a letter to a friend:

> I am still determined to be cheerful and to be happy in whatever situation I may be, for I have also learnt from experianence [sic] that the greater part of our happiness or misary [sic] depends upon our dispositions, and not upon our circumstances; we carry the seeds of the one, or the other about with us, in our minds, wherever we go.[42]

Martha made a conscious decision to choose positivity, and I remind myself that if she could do it, I can at least try! Holocaust survivor Viktor Frankl similarly said, "Everything can be taken from a man but one thing; the last of the human freedoms—to choose one's attitude in any given set of circumstances, to choose one's own way."[43] We *can* choose to embrace a positive attitude about our current circumstances when we resist complaining, celebrate gratitude, embrace a spirit of happiness, and choose to reframe our view of our circumstances.

Complaining is a spirit-draining, toxic, and unconscious habit which has very little, if any, benefit. My Coast Guard Academy classmates were aware of something that I was not: I was a complainer. Discovering this was one of the hardest lessons I've learned. During basic training at Coast Guard Academy in 1992, I felt thwarted by many things, and I found nearly everything, from memorizing facts and menus to running the obstacle course, difficult and uncomfortable. One day, our platoon commander tasked each of us to complete anonymous evaluations of one another. These assessment forms were called FOIE forms—ironically pronounced "phooey" and an acronym for Feedback on Interpersonal Effectiveness. I will never forget the day I received my stack of anonymous forms. They were relentlessly negative, biting, and consistent—I was a complainer, and my classmates were tired of it. I experienced a great deal of emotional pain from those forms and how the feedback was delivered, but I am grateful today for that invitation to be more mindful of how I perceive my circumstances and how

41. "Martha Washington Biography," paras. 3 and 6.
42. Washington, letter to Mercy Otis Warren, para. 2.
43. Frankl, *Man's Search*, 66.

I share that with others. While I continually feel the need to make "Stop complaining" one of my New Year's resolutions because I'm far from cured of my temptation to complain, I have saved a lot of emotional energy, mental bandwidth, and friendships due to this important realization and my effort to be more mindful of negativity in my thoughts and words.

In addition to resisting the temptation to complain, we can have a more positive experience of our present circumstances by working to discover and celebrate gratitude. Thich Nhat Hanh said, "The miracle is not to walk on water. The miracle is to walk on the green Earth in the present moment, to appreciate the peace and beauty that are available now."[44] Gratitude is the sense of appreciation, awe, and thankfulness for the beauty that we see, experience, or possess. This might seem an impossible task if one has endured suffering, yet Elie Wiesel, a Jewish scholar who suffered deeply during the Holocaust, said, "When a person doesn't have gratitude, something is missing in his or her humanity. A person can almost be defined by his or her attitude toward gratitude."[45] A spirit of gratitude enables us to see the good even in the most desperate circumstances.

We can also modify our view of our present circumstances by embracing a spirit of happiness. We might be irritated by the photo of a beautiful woman leaping in the air in a sunny field of wildflowers on the cover of my *Mayo Clinic Handbook for Happiness* because this image creates an expectation of happiness that is unrealistic and exaggerated. Many of us are far from realizing this euphoria even in our best moments. Nevertheless, working to embrace a spirit of happiness *will* benefit our resilience. The Dalai Lama asserts that the purpose of life is to seek happiness and that we can achieve happiness by "training the mind."[46] Happiness is not a superficial feeling inspired by accumulating wealth or accolades, but it is instead a product of our mindset, social connectedness, perspective, and practice. Gretchen Rubin, the author of *The Happiness Project*, offers one strategy: "One of the best ways to make *yourself* happy is to make other people happy; one of the best ways to make *other people* happy is to be happy yourself."[47] Although it seems like an endless circle, happiness is a mindset and can be "achieved

---

44. Nhat Hanh, *Touching Peace*, 1.
45. Wiesel, "Oprah Talks to Elie Wiesel," para. 2.
46. Dalai Lama and Cutler, *Art of Happiness*, 13–14.
47. Rubin, "Eight Splendid Truths," § "Second Splendid Truth."

by changing how you spend your time and your outlook on life."[48] We can strive to make happiness a habit.

Our outlook on life is ultimately a choice, and we can make the choice to reframe our perception of our circumstances in more positive ways. In a book entitled *The Art of Possibility*, the authors say, "Many of the circumstances that seem to block us in our daily lives may only appear to do so based on a framework of assumptions we carry with us. Draw a different frame around the same set of circumstances and new pathways come into view."[49]

At the Coast Guard Academy, I learned the importance of maintaining a healthy, realistic perspective on my life and seeing my cup as half full. The six weeks I spent aboard "America's tall ship" *Eagle* were among the most incredible and exhilarating of my life. The thrill of facing twenty-foot seas in the North Atlantic and exploring European cities were among the reasons I decided to attend the academy in the first place. These weeks were also among the most difficult of my life. The sexual harassment that other women and I experienced was consistent—from mocking the weight we gained to openly criticizing our strength and effort. At the end of the trip, a friend and I decided to file a formal sexual harassment complaint and initiated an investigation that resulted in the expulsion of one of my male classmates. The retaliation was swift and fierce; as I've been told, there was a gathering of male classmates who inventoried any evidence they had against those of us who initiated the report. Because there were so many regulations—as trivial as how we folded our underwear and what direction we fed our belts through our belt loops—almost everyone was guilty of something. In our case, we were guilty of socializing with the enlisted crewmembers during our *Eagle* deployment. I always found it challenging to see myself as somehow superior to the enlisted, and Lord knows I didn't feel comfortable socializing with my many of my male classmates. Still, it was an unambiguous rule, and I knowingly broke it. This resulted in my being punished with demerits (points that cadets would accumulate when they broke rules), restriction (basically house arrest), and many hours of marching tours (marching in dress uniform with our rifles around the perimeter of the barrack's courtyard). It was devastating, and the shame was deepened by the catcalls and derogatory shouts from the windows during

48. Grenville-Cleave, *Positive Psychology*, 6.
49. Stone Zander and Zander, *Art of Possibility*, 1.

my demeaning and public marching. I thought to myself, "Things could definitely *not* get worse." Was I ever wrong!

While on restriction, my friend and I were lying on the bed and lamenting our inability to leave the barracks to join our friends in town. An upperclassman came by the room to ensure we were complying with the terms of the punishment, which we weren't because we were required to be in uniform and were instead wearing gym clothes. To our shock, the charges against us were not limited to our failure to comply with the uniform regulations; we were accused of being gay. Sadly, there was a great deal of homophobia at the academy, and this accusation could have led to my involuntary discharge from the military. I suddenly went from thinking things couldn't get worse to publicly defending myself against this additional charge, living with the school-wide rumors and harassment that surrounded it, and facing possible expulsion. This chapter of my story did, however, have a happy conclusion, if you want to call it that. Although that incident intensified my sense of persecution and hopelessness, we were exonerated of the charge, and I learned an important lesson about perspective: things could always be worse.

Although that seems like a pessimistic viewpoint, studies show that comparing ourselves to those whose situations are more dire and tenuous actually helps modify our impressions of our own circumstances. Our perception and perspective matter. Since that time, I have found it helpful to imagine the many ways things *could* be worse and to appreciate that those things are not realities for me. I have spoken openly with my daughter about a miscarriage we suffered before the birth of her big brother. When she was about five, she sighed contentedly and innocently said, "I'm so glad that baby died." When I asked her to tell me more, she explained that she loves our family and realizes that she might not have been born had this baby come into this world as planned. Although it is still incredibly hard for me to see it that way, it helped me tremendously to see her childlike perception of it, which was unaffected by the emotions and heartbreak we experienced at that time. How we choose to view our circumstances makes a huge difference.

POSITIVITY IN OUR VIEW OF FUTURE CIRCUMSTANCES

In addition to identifying and celebrating the positive aspects of our past and present, how we perceive our future is also an important element of living more positively. We obviously have no way of knowing what is forthcoming in our lives and relationships. This is admittedly frustrating and unsettling, particularly for those of us who like to be in control. Our positivity and, ultimately, our resilience, will benefit if we are able to release some of our angst and anticipation about our future circumstances by avoiding worry, embracing optimism, and staying hopeful.

Worry attacks our capacity to be positive and is futile and unproductive. In a letter to John Adams, Thomas Jefferson said this:

> There are, indeed, (who might say nay) gloomy and hypochondriac minds, inhabitants of diseased bodies, disgusted with the present, and despairing of the future; always counting that the worst will happen, because it may happen. To these I say, how much pain have cost us the evils which have never happened! My temperament is sanguine. I steer my bark with Hope in the head, leaving Fear astern.[50]

In other words, we experience unnecessary fear and pain when we worry about events or outcomes that may never come to fruition. According to one study, only 8 percent of what we worry about actually happens, and of that, half of those things were beyond our control anyway.[51] Worry is an unproductive distraction, and it saps the emotional and spiritual energy we need to face hardship and disappointment. In the words attributed to the Dalai Lama, "If a problem is fixable, if a situation is such that you can do something about it, then there is no need to worry. If it's not fixable, then there is no help in worrying. There is no benefit in worrying whatsoever."[52] In a Bible study during my years at the academy, we were encouraged to memorize this verse from the Hebrew Bible: "Trust in the Lord with all your heart and lean not on your own understanding; in all your ways submit to him, and he will make your paths straight."[53] This verse has provided great comfort to me over the years, reminding me to relinquish control (well, at least some of it!), to reject worry, and to more boldly live into tomorrow with less worry weighing us down.

In addition to avoiding worry, embracing optimism helps us live a more positive life. Optimism is "an inclination to put the most favorable construction upon actions and events or to anticipate the best possible

50. Jefferson, Letter CXXX, to John Adams.

51. Sicinski, "Practical Ideas," § 3.

52. Dalai Lama, exact source unknown.

53. Prov 3:5–6 (NIV).

outcome."[54] It helps us look toward the future with enthusiasm and "serves as a fuel that ignites resilience and provides energy to power the other resilience factors."[55] Dietrich Bonhoeffer, a Lutheran pastor who was imprisoned and eventually executed for his opposition to the Nazi regime during World War II, addressed this issue in his writings from prison by saying the following:

> The essence of optimism is that it takes no account of the present, but it is a source of inspiration, of vitality and hope where others have resigned; it enables a man to hold his head high, to claim the future for himself and not to abandon it to his enemy.[56]

Even when things looked dire, Bonhoeffer determinedly lived with optimism. Being optimistic allows us to be more creative, resourceful, and hopeful.

Staying hopeful is another way to build our positivity and ultimately our resilience. Catholic theologian Henry Nouwen said that hope "makes it possible to look beyond the fulfillment of urgent wishes and pressing desires and offers a vision beyond human suffering and even death."[57] Hope allows us to endure hardship because of a belief that things will work out, even if they don't work out as we planned, and that the suffering will not last forever. As a hospice chaplain, it would sadden me when people would say, "The doctor said there is no hope." While some of us orient our hope on religious concepts such as Divine miracles, eternal life in heaven, or the belief that "all things work together for good,"[58] sources of hope abound for believers and nonbelievers alike. Perhaps the hope is not in an unlikely cure, but maybe instead the hope is in experiencing a comfortable and peaceful death, mending a broken relationship, spending quality time with family and friends, or simply laughing often. Hope is never obsolete, even during our most difficult challenges. In his letter to fledgling church in Rome found in the Christian New Testament, the apostle Paul said, "We also boast in our sufferings, knowing that suffering produces endurance, and endurance produces character, and character produces hope, and hope

---

54. *Merriam-Webster Online*, s.v. "Optimism," https://www.merriam-webster.com/dictionary/optimism.

55. Southwick and Charney, *Resilience*, 25.

56. Bonhoeffer, *Prisoner*, 25.

57. Nouwen, *Wounded Healer*, 76.

58. Rom 8:28 (NRSV).

does not disappoint us."[59] Hope is powerful and gives us great strength to persevere. An old proverb says, "The darkest hour is just before the dawn." Avoiding worry, embracing optimism, and staying hopeful can enable us to look at our future circumstances in a more positive way.

"FOCUS ON THE CLEAR PATH"

My perky and beloved academy classmate and friend Kate embraces positivity with authenticity and enthusiasm in every aspect of her life and has been an inspiration to me and many others. We met on a sunny day in July of 1992 at the Coast Guard Academy's Reporting-In-Day, when we were both among the several dozen "swabs" assigned to the platoon Whiskey-2. She was small, feisty, confident, and entirely determined to kick the crap out of the six weeks of basic training. The academy was all she ever wanted and was the only college to which she applied. On the other hand, I applied to a dozen schools and was intimidated by the whole experience. I arrived less prepared than I should have been, and I had no idea what I had gotten myself into. She and I ended up being crammed into a triple with a third woman and embarked upon what would be a life-changing six weeks for all of us.

It would have been fair for her to assume I would not last very long at the academy, and she would have been justified to assume I was going to be a liability for the platoon. While many of us found ourselves in that latter category at one point or another, I also frustrated her in other ways. One night, after mandatory "lights out," I was trimming my toenails in the dark while my roommates tried to fall asleep. Clip. Clip. Clip. After a few minutes, Kate lost her patience and ordered me to stop with an assertive whisper through gritted teeth. That speaks to the amount of stress we were under and the incredible focus and ability she demonstrated even from the very beginning of that rigorous program.

What I came to learn as our friendship grew was that she decided in seventh grade that she was going to attend the Coast Guard Academy. For the next six years, she surrounded herself with people who valued that goal and encouraged her, and she dismissed the opinions of her naysayers. She tackled one barrier after another, even just squeaking by in the medical intake exam because her height was just a fraction below the mandatory minimum (they thankfully rounded up!). What she lacked in stature she

59. Rom 5:3–5 (NRSV).

made up for in determination and positivity. She was confident and believed in herself. She never saw setbacks as failures or as indications that she was a bad performer or a bad person. She trusted herself. She looked out for others, seeing each of us as the whole and complex people we were, with both endearing and exasperating characteristics, but she chose to focus on the good attributes and qualities in each of us. She learned from the setbacks of her past, never complained, worked incredibly hard, and maintained her focus on the next assignment or task without becoming overwhelmed, debilitated by worry, or despondent. In May of 1996, her dream of becoming a Coast Guard officer came to fruition.

For Kate, being accepted to a service academy and graduating successfully helped prepare her for future challenges she could never have imagined facing. The day before the attack on the World Trade Center, Kate was heading to the airport after a meeting, wondering why people at the meeting were having a difficult time understanding her comments and suggestions and were continually asking her to repeat herself. She then called and left a voicemail for a friend who called back and asked, "I know you called, but what is wrong with you? You sound like you have marbles in your mouth." In a conversation with her mom a little later, her mom asked if she had been drinking. She made an appointment with the doctor and went the next day. The physicians ruled out various things, including multiple sclerosis, commonly called MS, though her odd symptoms continued over the next two years. During that time, she happened to meet a woman with MS in a purple wheelchair that was exercising with a trainer. She also met others living with MS and other physical challenges, and Kate became aware of how they were successfully managing their lives and developed a depth of empathy and understanding. By the time Kate heard the words "You have MS," she had a plan for how she would bravely live with this challenging illness.

MS is a condition in which a person's immune system attacks his or her own central nervous system, impacting the brain's ability to communicate with the body. Each individual's disease activity is different and unpredictable, but MS can lead to muscle weakness or spasms, vision and balance problems, difficulty swallowing and speaking, and even numbness and paralysis. Kate manages her MS by taking disease-modifying medication and deliberately focusing on her diet, exercise, sleep, exertion, and mental wellness. To manage her MS, her positive attitude has been essential. She decided that she wouldn't just live with MS, but she would give a voice to this disease—living with an openness and honesty that others might be afraid of doing for fear of the limitations others would put on them. She would become a proactive and loving parent and valued employee, she would train to be a competitive triathlete and create a robust and productive fundraising team, and she would dedicate herself to inspiring and uplifting others through writing, speaking, and social media. She embraces life, lives it fully, and is an inspiration to others due to her unfailing positivity.

Kate's positive attitude has been put to the test, however. Kate spent many months rigorously training for one of the hardest races in the country, the Ironman Lake Placid. Although its website describes the course as "serene," the race involves a grueling 2.4-mile swim, mountainous 112-mile bike, and an interminable 26.2-mile run, which requires as much as seventeen hours of full exertion. Kate's training was on schedule, but about six weeks before the race, she woke up to discover her skin was numb on one side. She was determined to keep training, but when she began seeing double, she was forced to dramatically change her training goals and regimen. Even with these seriously unfavorable symptoms, her unstoppable positive attitude (and a round of steroids!) helped get her to the starting line—and the finish line—that day and enabled her to reach a goal of becoming an Ironman Triathlete.

She is still racing and training, riding determinedly on a bike with the word "gratitude" on the top tube, but she needs to be intentional and mindful of her body. There are days when she needs to be conscious about how to walk, remembering to roll off her big toe. She admits to stumbling often when walking the halls of her office, but most often as she climbs the stairs, since she refuses to take the elevator. There are also a few shattered glasses and plates that slipped from her hands while washing dishes. She refuses to see these challenges as "adversity" or "setbacks," but she instead reframes difficulties as "upping the ante," inspiring her to dig deeper, giving her a deeper sense of accomplishment, and providing an opportunity for her to surprise herself. She said this in a speech to aspiring young female athletes:

> I am all for tackling challenges. Finding difficult races, picking the hardest job I can find. But when we call out these challenges as adverse conditions, we risk giving adversity too much power. As a cycling coach, I tell people when they see a pothole, to focus on the clear path around the pothole. By focusing where you want to go, you will avoid the pothole. If you freak out and keep staring at the pothole, you will nail it. Every time. By focusing on the

adverse conditions, you are focusing on the potholes, focusing on your perceived limitations.[60]

Kate does not deny that the potholes exist but she refuses to focus on them, recognizing that her attitude is essential. She quotes Henry Ford who said, "Whether you think you can or think you can't, you're right." Amazingly, she has come to see MS as "a bit of a blessing" because it has helped her slow down and prioritize. Positive thinking *can* and *does* change how we interact with the world and affects what we can accomplish.

FINAL THOUGHTS ON POSITIVITY

Embracing a positive attitude is doable. By focusing on our views of ourselves and others and our perceptions of our past, current, and future circumstances, we can make positive thinking a habit. Imagine two animals within you: one positive and one negative. When we continually feed the negative, it grows larger, stronger, and more aggressive. When we instead choose to feed the positive, the same can happen, with amazing results. When we release our anger, resentment, worry, despair, complaining, and hopelessness, we can embrace a spirit of positivity, daily choosing to celebrate love, forgiveness, trust, optimism, and hope. Do you think the glass is half empty or half full? Well, let's look at it this way: "People who wonder if the glass is half empty or half full miss the point. The glass is refillable."[61]

REFLECTION AND ACTION

Questions to ponder

- Take time to be mindful of "the bright side" of situations that seem frustrating or that do not go as planned. Take a few moment to consider how things could be worse and be grateful they are not.

- When and to whom do you complain? How could you channel that negative energy in different ways?

- When you face a problem, consider your instinct to see the problem as either overwhelming or manageable. If you tend to see problems as

---

60. Morse, "Overcoming Adversity."
61. Attributed to Simon Sinek, motivational speaker and author.

overwhelming, ask yourself what strategies might be helpful to you to break the problem down into smaller parts. If that is difficult for you, are there people you can enlist to help you do that?

- When are the times that you blame yourself when things do not go as planned? What different language could you use in your mind when you see that happening? If you are the type of person to apologize often, objectively take note of the occasions when it is truly your fault and times when you are taking too much responsibility.

- When have you solved a problem that you thought might have been too challenging to execute? When have you seen yourself exhibiting a "can-do" attitude about ideas and projects?

- When do you use sarcasm when communicating with others? How is it helpful to you? How is it costing you? What is it providing you?

- How do you feel after spending time on social media? Happy, drained, frustrated, or distracted? How is your interaction with social media helping or hurting your pursuit of positivity?

Strategies for cultivating this characteristic of resilience

- Once or twice a week, document and explore things for which you are grateful, both things that you are grateful for having or experiencing, as well as those things you are grateful that you do *not* have or experience.

- Limit your time on social media and carefully manage the time you spend reading articles about issues that you find frustrating or infuriating, particularly if the content is not explicitly clarifying or helpful.

- Keep a small pad near a jar, jot down things for which you are grateful, and put them into the jar. Read the notes of gratitude when you are having a bad day or at the end of the week, month, or year.

- Recite positive affirmations in the mirror each day such as "I am beloved" or "I am strong" or "I am enough."

- Volunteer in a capacity that gives you joy, perhaps in a role that involves helping people or animals.

- Be unexpectedly kind to someone or "pay it forward."

- Smile intentionally for no reason.

- Make a collage of things you are grateful for using cutouts from magazines or newspapers.

- Before each meal, have everyone share something for which they are grateful or the highlight of their day or week.

- Journal about negative experiences in your life, since the process of writing often helps process and organize events in ways that perseverating about them does not.[62] When you are done, try not to overthink these negative thoughts or experiences.

- Journal or ponder about situations or individuals that are struggling more than you as a way of recognizing the ways in which things could be worse.[63]

- Establish a positive mantra for yourself and recite it when you are feeling stressed or disappointed, such as "I am doing a good job" or "I'm using my gifts the best I can" or "I am a hard worker."

- When you are reminiscing with family or friends, try to remember and celebrate positive events and interactions instead of—or in addition to—negative ones.

Prayer

God of Hope and the Rising Sun, you are our companion and light when we are in dark times. Please help to clear away those things getting in the way of our positivity. Help us to recognize our own uniqueness and our own giftedness, remembering that we were created by you in your image, knitted together in our mothers' wombs. Invite us to recognize the gifts and skills you have given us and the ways we bring light to the world. Create in us spirits of generosity and love for others, even those who are frustrating and difficult to love. Enable us to give people the benefit of the doubt and to forgive others, even when they don't deserve it. When we are able to be kind and forgiving, please teach us ways to protect ourselves from further hurt and the courage to follow through. Help us, Loving God, to look upon our past and discover and celebrate the gems of joy, peace, and contentment, even amid the difficulties and sadness. In the present moment, walk with

62. Grenville-Cleave, *Positive Psychology*, 154.
63. Dalai Lama and Cutler, *Art of Happiness*, 23.

us so that we can resist complaining and reframe our circumstances. Help open our eyes and hearts so that we might discover gratitude and happiness. Finally, enter our fretful minds with your peace, and fill our hearts and spirits with hope for the future, so today is not full of angst or dread for tomorrow. May we embrace and live more positively, radiating the light of your love and peace. Amen.

3

Pliability

Whatever is flexible and flowing will tend to grow.
Whatever is rigid and blocked will atrophy and die.

—Lao Tzu[1]

"Life is flux." As much as we might wish the cynical Greek philosopher Heraclitus was wrong, change is unavoidable. When we survive a traumatic event, personal loss, chronic marginalization, systemic bias, or a one-time failure, unwanted and unexpected change *will* occur. Change has the ability to cause emotional, spiritual, and even physical suffering. In the midst of experiencing change, we are faced with uncertainty, insecurity, and new understandings of ourselves and our circumstances. The healthiest way to manage change is to embrace a spirit of *Pliability*. A friend named David, a social worker from the Buddhist tradition, once shared this insightful quote during one of our hospice team meetings: "The patients and families who experience the dying process with the greatest peace are those most adaptable to change."[2] This is because we often experience change when we undergo hardship, and we often undergo hardship when we experience change. Being pliable, or flexible, is key to resilience because embracing change helps reduce our suffering.

1. Lao Tzu, quoted in Heider, *Tao of Leadership*, § 76.
2. David Gibbs (social worker), conversation with author, circa 2006.

As a college chaplain, I regularly see my students wrestle with the pain associated with change. Young adulthood is a time of complex and relentless change, and many students visit me with symptoms of insomnia, an inability to focus, and debilitating anxiety that are directly related to the many changes they experience or anticipate. Whether the change is positive or negative, I notice these same symptoms because change, even when it is a change for the better, is incredibly hard.

When I resigned from the Coast Guard, for instance, I was an emotional wreck. I knew in my mind that my discharge would serve as a liberation from the distress I experienced while serving, but my heart and spirit were filled with angst, grief, and the pernicious "what if" questions. At that point, I could only think of the many things I loved about my maritime service and not those things that were toxic and precipitated my resignation. I was full of grief and resentment over the changes I was experiencing.

As a devout person of faith, perhaps I should have been more comfortable with change because flexibility is addressed and celebrated by many different religious and spiritual traditions. The prophet to whom the Qur'an was revealed, Muhammad, peace be upon him, stated this: "In the face of the storms of events the position of a believer is like a flexible plant. When a stormy wind hits, it shows softness and does not remain stiffly erect."[3] Muhammad also expertly role-modeled flexibility while negotiating treaties, even to the point of being criticized by some who would have been inclined to take a more rigid and unbending approach.[4] Similarly, various religious traditions share stories of people faced with changing circumstances, difficulties, and strife who demonstrated productive and meaningful adaptability, including Abraham, Jesus, Mary, the Dalai Lama, Moses, and Guru Nanak. While there are role models everywhere of people embracing change with pliability, pliability is sometimes misunderstood.

WHAT PLIABILITY IS NOT

Pliability requires open-mindedness, but being pliable does *not* require us to compromise what we believe. South African activist and politician Nelson Mandela was successful and persistent because of his spirit of flexibility. In the forties and fifties, Mandela participated in a movement that called attention to racial injustice in South Africa. In the early sixties, he was

3. Muhammad (pbuh), quoted in "Flexibility," para. 6.
4. "Flexibility," para. 8.

incarcerated in a South African prison, after almost being executed.[5] After nearly thirty years, the culture became more receptive to his political beliefs, and he was finally released and elected the president of the country that once persecuted him. One scholar cites his pliability in saying that Mandela's effectiveness was "most evident in the patient and flexible pragmatism which kept going the cause of South African liberal democracy as against its many detractors."[6] He was strategic and intentional, open-minded and adaptable, which ultimately gave him the strength and power to help initiate much-needed change without compromising his beliefs. While in prison, Nelson Mandela refused release *several times* because he was unwilling to agree to the terms that would have required him to concede his values.[7] Yet he found unlikely partners and adjusted his strategies throughout his decades of advocacy, showing he could have both strong convictions *and* flexibility. The treasured skills of finding shared goals, relenting on aspects of our plan or intentions that are nonessential, and finding common ground are skills that are becoming scarce, and a willingness to embrace a spirit of pliability will enable us to experience more peace as we endure the difficulties of life.

Being pliable does not require us to compromise our beliefs, and it also has *nothing* to do with giving up. We can be a flexible plant without allowing ourselves to be uprooted or denuded. Whether it be in the political sphere, in our relationships, or in our advocacy, embracing change and being flexible are signs of strength and realism, not signs of cowardice or weakness. In hospice, I sometimes heard patients or families describe their transition from active treatment to hospice care as "giving up" because hospice care typically provides comfort care and symptom management instead of aggressive active treatment. This choice to transition to hospice care was definitely not "giving up," but it was often a practical and reality-informed decision that showed healthy pliability. It allowed patients to focus on creating quality time with their families that was blessed, fulfilling, peaceful, comfortable, and joy filled. These patients did not give up, but they instead shifted their focus in healthy and life-affirming ways.

Sadly, pliability is sometimes characterized as a character flaw, which it is *not*. We hear accusations of "flip flopping" when people might rationally

5. *Encyclopaedia Britannica Online*, s.v. "Nelson Mandela," https://www.britannica.com/biography/Nelson-Mandela.

6. Spear, "Nelson Mandela's Genius," para. 6.

7. *Encyclopaedia Britannica Online*, s.v. "Nelson Mandela," https://www.britannica.com/biography/Nelson-Mandela.

rethink their positions on issues. We hear charges of weakness or resignation when people just might choose to spend their energy in different or more productive ways. Flexible people are sometimes thought to be short on conviction, to lack resolve, or to give in easily, but circumstances and details sometimes evolve, and the ability to adapt, reassess, and adjust is a critically essential and beneficial skill. Pliability is this: a willingness to acknowledge the new realities we face and to mindfully and intentionally live into those realities by reserving judgment, managing anxiety, and embracing hope.

ACKNOWLEDGING THE NEW REALITY

The first step in embracing pliability is to identify the changes we are experiencing. Undergoing trauma or difficulty causes "inner reorientation and self-redefinition"[8] and has the power to affect our identity and how we interact with the world. While our employers, colleagues, and friends sometimes expect us to compartmentalize, we bring grief and stress into all aspects of our lives, and we live differently when we lose a loved one, a job, or our sense of safety and security. Perhaps we now identify as a survivor, divorcée, or widow. Reverend Donna Schaper relates these changes to the Christian Bible, which says, "Now those who had been scattered by the persecution that broke out when Stephen was killed traveled as far as Phoenicia, Cyprus and Antioch."[9] She acknowledges that when we suffer trauma or persecution, we may not be geographically scattered, but we may become emotionally scattered. She said this:

> That is persecution's worst feature: it goes on forever. Once you are beaten up on the street as a gay teenager, you look at streets in a different way. Once raped, you look at sex a different way. Once beaten up, you find that you can't really stay in good enough shape. Persecution scatters us.[10]

Our minds and spirits may feel scattered and broken, and it is not possible to get back to that point prior to our unwanted "awakening." Evidence of this can be seen in the concept of the "depression-era mentality." Many who survived the Great Depression were forever worried and anxious

8. Bridges, *Transitions*, xii.

9. Acts 11:19 (NIV).

10. Schaper, "Scattered," 7.

about scarcity and poverty, no matter how far they came from their time of desperate wanting. Even if their fortunes were restored, many were never able to look at money with the same flippancy or take financial security for granted, and some even passed this new worldview and anxiety on to their children. In his book *Transitions*, William Bridges says, "We feel these unexpected losses [of our previous identities] because, to an extent that we seldom realize, we come to identify ourselves with the circumstances of our lives."[11] Trauma and difficulty change who we are and how we see ourselves.

In addition to changes to ourselves as individuals, hardship and trauma also cause concrete and direct changes to our life circumstances. When we lose a loved one, for instance, there are changes to our family, our routines, and our relationships, and even perhaps changes to our housing and financial situations. When we lose a job, we might lose a sense of social connection with friends, our fiscal security, and our sense of purpose. Life will not be the same, as much as we might want that. Even when the change results from our own initiative, change is deeply challenging. We see this in the lives of women with abusive partners. Some critics wonder why the women don't simply leave the relationship, but anyone who has had an abusive partner or supported a person in that position realizes the complexity, danger, financial insecurity, guilt, fear, shame, and other profound consequences that may be associated with the change related to a separation or divorce. Author and advocate Kay Schubach, for instance, speaks publicly about how hard it was to leave her abusive and controlling husband, even after his terrifying threats and his attempt to physically smother her. Kay talked about the investment she made in the relationship and the things they shared, all the things that would change if she chose to leave.[12] Change is hard, even when it is for the better, even when it is desperately necessary.

Challenges related to changing identity and circumstances are even evident in "military reintegration," the occasions when service members return from deployment and rejoin their families. Families learned to function with their loved ones absent, and long durations away from home make desperately longed-for reunifications surprisingly awkward. Although the "reintegration" is a change for the better, the high expectations of the reunion are unlikely to be met, and families often struggle as service members return home and try to rediscover their places within their relationships and family units. Living into our changed identities

11. Bridges, *Transitions*, 12.

12. Davey, "Most Dangerous Time," § "Kay Schubach," para. 13.

and circumstances can be challenging. Physicians and researchers Dennis Charney and Stephen Southwick say, "Accepting the reality of our situation, even if that situation is frightening or painful, is an important component of cognitive flexibility" and allows us to "acknowledge, rather than ignore, potential roadblocks."[13] Mindfully and intentionally living into the new reality will enable us to cope most successfully.

LIVING INTO THE NEW REALITY

Once we acknowledge the changes we are experiencing, mindfully and intentionally living into the new reality helps enhance our resilience. A strategy for living into our new reality is articulated so beautifully by the Reformed theologian Reinhold Niebuhr's Serenity Prayer, one of the simplest yet most profound prayers we can utter: "God grant me the serenity to accept the things I cannot change; courage to change the things I can; and wisdom to know the difference." Pliability is necessary to "accept the things we cannot change" because we must have flexibility in our attitudes and mindsets. Pliability is also essential to "change the things we can," since doing so requires us to creatively take initiative and make adjustments and modifications to our lives and circumstances.

When we are ready, taking an inventory of ourselves and our circumstances will allow us to be honest about ways in which the hardship changed us and our lives, while honoring the feelings of grief over the things that will not be the same. Doing this inventory will enable us to identify the changes over which we have little power, where we might need assistance from others, aspects of our circumstances that we can repair or improve, and things we may need to do differently. Living into the new reality can be very challenging, particularly because that new reality is unknown and often unwanted, but intentionally recognizing the changes and boldly living into them with pliability is ultimately a beneficial choice.

Accepting what we cannot change is essential. To live into our new reality, it is necessary to take our focus off wanting things to be just as they were. Simply wishing change has not happened ineffectively drains a tremendous amount of finite, critical energy, preventing us from working on being more resilient and on finding solutions. It also torments the soul, enhancing our grief and lament. A friend told me a story about an aging couple she knew. The husband's condition began to deteriorate, and

13. Southwick and Charney, *Resilience*, 169.

he was unable to do many of the things they did as a couple. The wife was frustrated, disappointed, and sad. Eventually, the husband needed the bathroom to be refitted to be handicap accessible. The wife refused to make the modifications, even though there were no financial concerns preventing it, perhaps because she subconsciously would be admitting to his decline and thought she was allowing him to give up. Although the new reality was quite real, the denial of that new reality and the refusal to live into it made both partners in this relationship miserable and even put the husband at great physical risk. Even when the new reality is painful or unwanted, it is what it is, and living into that reality will save essential energy and enhance our resilience.

Just as our eyes adjust to darkness, accepting what we cannot change enables us to reserve essential energy for the task of living into the new reality. As a hospice chaplain, I was a spiritual companion for those who confronted what is probably the greatest change each of us must someday face—death itself. One of my primary jobs was to help people live into the changes they were experiencing. One middle-aged man was in the last stages of a terminal illness and was wheelchair bound from weakness. His symptoms eventually required him to move from his home in his beloved neighborhood to our inpatient facility. He could have just floundered in his grief about his physical limitations, but he didn't. He continued to live life to its fullest, finding joy in every day. In fact, he spoke with the team about the pleasure he experienced when attending the annual town-wide fair and eating the fair's famous "chop suey sandwich," which was literally Chinese chop suey on a bun. He inquired about going, and he was soon bundled up and transported by wheelchair bus to the fair where he ate his last chop suey sandwich with a huge smile on his face. He relished each bite of his unique sandwich, surrounded by the sounds and noises and smells of the festival, while he gladly remembered the many years of ritual, family memories, and joy. He resisted the temptation to be singularly focused on what he could *not* do and how this time was different. He instead focused on what he *could* do, and he died peacefully several weeks later. Accepting what we cannot change is a key to being resilient, but the Serenity Prayer does not end with "accept the things I cannot change." An essential piece of it is "the courage to change the things I can."

Realizing the power we *do* have to change our circumstances, even amid challenges, is empowering and benefits our resilience. An example of someone who showed pliability and took the initiative to change his circumstances is Abraham Lincoln, who was born in Kentucky to a low-income family. He suffered the loss of his mom when he was only nine years old. He spent his childhood in the woods, laboring on the farm and working to educate himself with whatever material he could scrounge up. He was familiar with grief; his sister died while giving birth when Lincoln was still just a teenager, and though he married and had four children, three of them died at young ages.[14] As if these life circumstances weren't difficult enough, Lincoln also suffered terribly from depression. In a letter to a friend, he said this: "I am now the most miserable man living. If what I feel were equally distributed to the whole human family, there would not be one cheerful face on the earth . . . To remain as I am is impossible; I must die or be better, it appears to me."[15]

In spite of these griefs and challenges, Abraham Lincoln was an effective lawyer and politician, and as the sixteenth president, was responsible for saving the union and putting into effect the Emancipation Proclamation. He acknowledged the realities in his life, and while he was powerless over some of his circumstances, he took incredible initiative and demonstrated flexibility by reading, learning, and working hard, eventually going on to live a fulfilling and influential life. There is a saying: "We cannot make the wind blow, but we can adjust our sails in obedience to the laws of the wind, and they immediately give us their power to go where we will."[16] Whether or not we have power over the circumstances of our lives, we have the ability to live into the new reality with resiliency by reserving judgment of ourselves and our circumstances, managing our anxiety, and embracing hope.

Reserving judgment

Judging ourselves and our circumstances takes emotional energy and cognitive bandwidth. Judging our situations does not change them; instead, it uses energy that could otherwise be used to help us be prepared for and transformed by hardship—to cultivate the characteristics that help us be more resilient. As Maya Angelou said, "If you don't like something, change it. If you can't change it, change your attitude."[17] When events happen in our

14. "Lincoln Family Timeline."
15. Lincoln, letter to John T. Stuart, 1:229.
16. Johnson, *Studies in God's Methods*, 13.
17. "Maya Angelou," quote 2.

lives, we can resist immediately judging them by avoiding binary good/bad thinking and by rejecting "why me" thinking.

Admittedly, it is tempting to immediately and heartily judge events in our lives as good or bad. Binary good/bad thinking prevents us from seeing the complexities of life. There is great wisdom in this old Taoist tale:

> There was old farmer who farmed his fields for many years. One day his horse got away and ran off. When his neighbors heard the news, they came to him and said with sympathy, "Such bad luck!" "Maybe," the farmer calmly replied. To the farmer's surprise, the horse returned the next day and brought with it three other wild horses. "Such good luck!" the neighbors shouted joyfully. "Maybe," replied the wise old man. Early the next morning, the farmer's son was thrown off while trying to train one of the untamed horses and broke his leg. Again, the concerned neighbors gathered and said, "What bad luck!" "Maybe," the farmer said patiently. The following day, officials from the military visited the village to draft young men into the army. They left the son behind because of his broken leg. "What good luck!" the neighbors exclaimed. "Maybe," said the farmer. [18]

Like this farmer, as we look back at our lives, we may see different events that we thought were bad and turned out to be good and things we thought were good and were actually fairly bad. There may also be experiences that are so painful, no amount of good outcomes could possibly make up for the grief and sadness associated with it. In each of these scenarios, the story of the farmer's luck invites us to embrace a spirit of pliability that allows us to keep open the door of hope, even if just a crack. We can remain open to the possibility that good things sometimes take root in difficult circumstances—perhaps in the mending of a relationship, the growing of our faith, the discovery of inner strength, or the opening of another door. In the moment, we do not have the luxury of time and perspective because we see only a small piece of the picture and not its whole context. Similar to the farmer's story, the long-term outcomes of the discrete events in our lives are hard to anticipate and just might lead to blessing.

When we avoid binary good/bad thinking, we remain open to experiencing whatever unforeseen positive thing, however small, may result from our circumstances. One of my favorite people was a hospice patient of mine who was in her mid-nineties. As her illness progressed, she began to lose

---

18. Original source unknown.

her hearing and became weaker. A disappointing milestone was her losing her ability to knit fine, detailed items, a cherished life-long hobby that
helped satisfy her creative energy. That did not stop her. She continued to
knit with increasingly large knitting needles while continuing to enjoy the
simple pleasures of life like visits from her family and conversations with
the hospice team. Even when knitting became impossible, she expressed her
creativity by making drawings on a white board with her hospice volunteer.
Although her life and level of functioning were changing for the worse, she
looked at the new reality and lived fully and generously in it. She was flexible, and she mindfully adjusted her expectations and projects based on her
diminishing abilities. She was able to stay connected to creative activities
that were spiritually life-giving for her. Her buoyed spirit gave her extra
energy to spend with her family and friends, making her last months and
weeks fulfilling and peaceful. She proactively found ways to enjoy her life in
different and new ways and reserved judgment of herself and her circumstances. When we acknowledge our new reality, we can imitate her example
of flexibility and live into it.

In addition to resisting binary good/bad thinking, we also benefit from
rejecting "why me" thinking. It is so tempting and natural to ask, "Why
me?" when we suffer the end of a relationship, experience violence, receive
a pink slip, face unwanted changes to our living situation, lose someone we
love, or hear a "no" when we desperately wanted to hear a "yes." Rabbi Harold Kushner's book *Why Bad Things Happen to Good People* aims to address
the puzzling "why me?" question.[19] Following the death of his fourteen-
year-old son Aaron, Rabbi Kushner explored the faith-shaking reality that
hardship falls upon both the good and the evil. Good people are not exempt
from suffering. He concluded that while God does not *cause* bad things to
happen to us, God is present with us in the suffering. In reality, each of us
is susceptible to trauma, difficulty, and hurt, regardless of how hard we try
to protect ourselves, avoid danger, prepare for every contingency, or stay on
God's "good side." Hardship and change are unavoidable, whoever we are.
As Jesus says of God in the Christian New Testament: "For he makes his
sun to shine on bad and good people alike, and gives rain to those who do
good and to those who do evil."[20]

In facing hardship, we will be better prepared for inevitable challenges if we reserve judgment of ourselves and our circumstances. As each

19. Kushner, *When Bad Things Happen.*

20. Matt 5:45 (GNT).

scenario passed him by, the farmer in the Taoist story acknowledged the realities and declined to overthink them, second guess himself, or dwell on what happened. He saved a lot of energy and some sanity! If only we could internalize these words from a letter Ralph Waldo Emerson wrote to one of his daughters:

> Finish every day and be done with it. For manners and for wise living it is a vice to remember. You have done what you could; some blunders and absurdities no doubt crept in; forget them as soon as you can. Tomorrow is a new day; you shall begin it well and serenely, and with too high a spirit to be cumbered with your old nonsense. This day for all that is good and fair. It is too dear, with its hopes and invitations, to waste a moment on the rotten yesterdays.[21]

Instead of lamenting the "rotten yesterdays," we can work to reserve judgment of our circumstances by rejecting binary good/bad thinking and resisting asking "Why me." Meanwhile, we benefit from being mindful of the anxiety that naturally accompanies the changes we may experience or anticipate.

Managing our anxiety

Anxiety hinders our ability to be pliable and is a significant and worsening issue in our society. In a recent study, 22 percent of college students reported feeling "overwhelming anxiety" in the past year, while less than 1 percent was diagnosed or seeking treatment for it.[22] We are less resilient when we are disabled by or hindered by anxiety. Connecting with mental health professionals can help us identify strategies for managing our anxiety and determine if medicine and therapy might help. Meanwhile, we can better manage our anxiety by being mindful of "what if" thinking, worry, and perfectionism.

We can reduce anxiety by resisting exaggerated "what if" thinking. "What if" thinking is a waste of time and risks sending us into spirals of angst and impotence. Instead, we can work to look at the situation that presents itself without imagining the many terrible or worrisome possibilities that are unlikely to ever come to pass. One cold spring evening, I was

---

21. Emerson, quoted in Cabot, *Memoir*, 2:489
22. "American College Health Association," 33–34.

home with my six-month-old baby when the doorbell rang. Facing me was a uniformed police officer looking quite serious, with black rubber gloves on his hands. Within seconds, I assumed my husband had been in a fatal accident on his way home from work, and I began trying to imagine what my life would be like without him. The officer asked if we were okay and said someone at my address called 911 from our home phone. I looked down at my baby Elsie in my arms. She was still holding our cordless phone in her hands and was entertaining herself by pressing the numbers. The officer looked at her with a smirk and said with a sweet voice, "I think I know who the culprit is." Although this has become just a funny story my daughter enjoys hearing retold, it was not funny to me in the moment. I clearly would have been much better off had I simply waited to hear what the officer had to say instead of imagining the worst! "What if" thinking is wasteful and even dangerous, and it is often associated with worry.

We can also reduce our anxiety by avoiding the downward spiral of worry, which is addressed in more detail in chapter 2. Worry is the "chain of thoughts and images, negatively affect-laden and relatively uncontrollable," that compromise our physical and mental wellness.[23] Ultimately, worry is simply an indicator of a problem needing to be addressed. In escaping the spiral and recognizing the problem, we are far more likely to be able to discern that critical piece of Niebuhr's prayer: the wisdom to know the difference between what we can change and what we cannot. Without making that distinction, we risk squandering essential energy worrying about things in the latter category—those things over which we have no control or influence. For those things we do have the power to change, we can turn worry into motivation, as long as we aren't held back by fear of imperfection.

Perfectionism joins "what if" thinking and worry to form the trifecta of obstacles that contribute to our anxiety and compromise our pliability—and ultimately our resilience. As a college chaplain, I often see the intense pressure students put on themselves to be perfect, which begins long before their college years. Rejecting perfectionism and embracing failure will benefit our resilience. Those of us dedicated to working in higher education commiserate about our concern that students are taking fewer academic risks and are opting for easier paths in order to avoid failure. My colleague Jen came up with a wonderful idea—programs that celebrate failure. She gathers students together and invites the faculty and staff to share their

23. Borkovec et al., quoted in Versluis et al., "Reducing Worry, 319.

stories of overcoming failure. One of the professors spoke about failing out of college the first time he tried it, which came a shock to the students who have such deep respect for him and his intelligence. It is powerful for the students to hear stories of successful, happy professionals who showed pliability and prevailed in spite of mistakes, misfortune, hardship, or bad choices. Some experts argue that failing is actually an essential part of success. In the popular book *The 21 Irrefutable Laws of Leadership*, John Maxwell says, "Every past success and failure you've experienced can be a valuable source of information and wisdom—if you allow it to be."[24] Rejecting the urge for "what if" thinking, worry, and perfectionism will help us to manage our anxiety and make us more resilient. When we are able to reduce our anxiety, our hearts are open to embracing a spirit of hope.

Embracing hope

Hope allows us to live into our new reality with a spirit of openness and optimism. We have hope in our hearts that our pain will eventually dissipate, our relationships will help bolster us, and we will become stronger, more capable, and more loving as a result of what we experience. My mentor, Reverend Robert Cotter, was a pastor and psychologist, and he often shared the story of the caterpillar's transformation into a butterfly. Many observers, and even possibly the caterpillar itself, would imagine that the story would have a sad ending. It seems hopeless as it sits stagnant and trapped for so long within its chrysalis. Yet when it emerges as a beautiful butterfly, we see transformation, beauty, and hope.

On a women's retreat recently, a participant named Gabriela provided another beautiful analogy. She sees the difficulties of life as manure. Yes, manure is mucky and foul smelling, but she appreciates that manure is rich, life-giving material. In it, beautiful flowers can grow, as in the Buddhist saying, "No mud, no lotus." She trusts that goodness can grow out of the "manure" of life. She has hope. The words from the prophet Jeremiah are comforting: "'For surely I know the plans I have for you,' says the Lord, 'plans for your welfare and not for harm, to give you a future with hope.'"[25] So as we engage in "the natural process of disorientation and reorientation" associated with changes resulting from hardship or trauma,[26] let us em-

---

24. Maxwell, *Laws of Leadership*, 39.

25. Jer 29:11 (NRSV).

26. Bridges, *Transitions*, 4.

brace pliability; doing so *is* a choice. Like a baby leaving the warm and safe womb and coming into the world, our reality might be changing whether we like it or not, but there are rich, fulfilling, and exciting opportunities ahead. We *can* and *will* survive and thrive.

"RESETTING GOALS IS A SIGN OF PROGRESS, NOT A SETBACK"

Rachelle is a woman of tremendous emotional, spiritual, and physical strength. I am not exaggerating about her physical strength; she is literally a professional bodybuilder, but the excellent health, self-respect, self-confidence, and strength she discovered and honed over the years does not overshadow her kindness, compassion, humbleness, wisdom, and gentleness. Rachelle has faced a variety of traumas and struggles throughout her life, and even as a self-identified Type-A personality, her pliability and adaptability have absolutely been essential to her success and happiness. She has learned to identify and live into the new realities she has faced with grace and hope, particularly as she left home after high school, experienced the ending of relationships, and underwent professional transitions.

While some of us struggled with homesickness, Rachelle was glad to report to the Coast Guard Academy in 1992 and welcomed the comprehensive, year-round program. Although she had a positive high school experience, her home life was distressing as she endured a great deal of physical violence at the hands of her stepfather. Because of her inner strength and wisdom, she rejected "why me" thinking and intentionally created a path for herself where she could be independent and self-sufficient. She had no intention of squandering this opportunity to "escape," so she worked incredibly hard to achieve academically and militarily at the academy and did so with grace and success as she worked to find her place in this new and unique context, particularly as a woman of color in a predominantly white male environment. Her ability to cut ties with her family of origin and adapt to military life required her to be flexible, and even though there were times she felt judged by others, she has a level of self-respect and self-esteem that has allowed her to trust in her choices and maintain hope in her future.

Rachelle's flexibility has also been put to the test in the ending of some significant romantic relationships. These transitions have been hard for her, particularly in light of her desire to settle down and have a family and in the fact that she feels judged by society for her singleness. Wisely, Rachelle recognizes that while pliability is an essential component of resilience, it does not mean that she should settle for less than she deserves. Even after investing a great deal into one specific relationship, she recognized that her boyfriend was becoming physically and emotionally abusive, and she bravely ended the relationship to keep herself safe and healthy. Listening to her intuition gave her the emotional and mental strength and flexibility to change course, even though she longed to be in a meaningful relationship.

Alongside these changes in her family life and in her romantic relationships, Rachelle has also experienced a variety of professional transitions. At one point in her Coast Guard career, she took a position that allowed her some geographic stability, even though she knew that it might hinder her ability to get promoted. When time came for promotion, taking that "career-killing" position did prove to be a liability, and she was forced to retire because of the "up or out" system in the military. She loved her service in the Coast Guard and had to reinvent her identity when she left because her sense of self had become so intertwined with her military service.

That change was challenging, but Rachelle lived into her new identity with grit and enthusiasm and pursued her passion to be a health educator and life coach. After several successful years in her professional wellness career, a job opportunity that appeared to offer promising opportunities for growth and generous compensation presented itself. She took yet another leap of faith to explore the unknown. She worked hard in this position but soon recognized that her boss was mistreating her professionally, which began to negatively compromise her physical and mental health and her well-being. Rachelle mustered up the strength and courage to look for a new job. She applied to and accepted a previous job despite judgment from colleagues who thought she was "giving up" or taking a step "backwards." Wisely, she returned to her mantra—a quote posted on her wall that reads, "Resetting goals is a sign of progress, not a setback." As Rachelle navigated through these voluntary and involuntary transitions, she chose to be loving, forgiving, and accepting of herself and others as she discovered ways to manage stress and anxiety in helpful and productive ways.

Rachelle's ability to survive hardships and challenges has helped her trust in her own strength, wisdom, and purpose. She does not judge herself or her circumstances and works hard to be, in her words: "the best person I can be: the best sister, daughter, friend, and human being in general." She recognizes that people might judge her and is able to cite examples of when people made judgments about her that proved untrue, but she has discovered a self-love and appreciation that stems from making her physical, spiritual, and emotional wellness a priority. Consistently, hope has been key for Rachelle. She has a strong faith that rests in the belief that everything happens for a reason, and she trusts that everything works out in the end. She has found peace even in phases of unknowing and uncertainty, knowing that God's plan for her will eventually be revealed.

Perhaps the most beautiful way she has demonstrated pliability came recently in her willingness and ability to discover empathy for her abusive stepfather. She has learned that he was likely suffering from untreated PTSD resulting from his military service in Vietnam, and he has lived in a culture where seeking mental health treatment was unacceptable. She has been able to forgive him and to appreciate the things he was able to provide. Her beautiful and loving spirit has allowed her to live with an openness to grace, possibilities, and hope. She is an incredible woman and beautifully illustrates that strength and pliability are definitely *not* mutually exclusive.

FINAL THOUGHTS ON PLIABILITY

Being pliable is key to resilience. Hardship and change go hand in hand. Let's learn to embrace change. Roman emperor Marcus Aurelius said it well: "All these things, which thou seest, change immediately and will no longer be; and constantly bear in mind how many of these changes thou hast already witnessed. The universe is transformation: life is opinion."[27] Because life itself is change, it can be argued that denying change is "a kind of death in that the individual is refusing to participate in that which defines life."[28] We must move from a mindset of resistance to a mindset of embrace. Let us live into change boldly and fearlessly, and may we brave these inescapable changes by acknowledging the new reality and by living into the new reality by reserving judgment, managing anxiety, and embracing hope.

27. Marcus Aurelius, *Meditations*, bk. 4, para. 4.
28. Mark, "Heraclitus," § "Heraclitus' World Order – Logos."

REFLECTION AND ACTION

Questions to ponder

- Reflect on an experience handling change and transition. What did you do well and where could you improve?

- What do you like about change? Identify changes in your past that you enjoyed and reflect on why you enjoyed them.

- What spontaneous things have you done lately? What do you enjoy about being spontaneous, and what aspects of spontaneity are challenging for you?

- If you are you inclined to judge circumstances as "good" or "bad," how can you be mindful of ways that your circumstances could be better or worse?

- If you struggle to maintain an open mind when change is thrust upon you, how can you incorporate new approaches? What mantras might be helpful in inviting your mind to remain open to possibilities?

- Reflect on your relationship with a counselor or therapist with whom you can process events and feelings of anxiety and worry. If you have trouble identifying that person, what can you do to develop these relationships?

- How is hope addressed by your theological or spiritual framework? How does it inspire or comfort you? Which quotes or versus are comforting to you?

Strategies for cultivating this characteristic of resilience

- Read the Taoist tale entitled "The Farmer's Luck," and rewrite the story using events from your life.

- Journal about times when something you thought would be a bad thing turned out to be a good thing and vice versa, or journal about times when new things emerged as a result of something else ending.

- Practice being mindful of your immediate judgment of circumstances, gently dismissing those judgments from your mind, and living into your circumstances with an open spirit.

- Journal about examples of when you adapted well to an unexpected circumstance or change. What helped you peacefully live into the new reality?

- If you are finding a certain change stressful, journal about the other aspects of your life that are constant and unchanging.

- Connect with people who have undergone similar changes, perhaps in a support group.

- Establish a mantra to help manage the change such as, "It is what it is."

- Connect with a therapist or counselor to identify and work through the changes associated with hardship or trauma, particularly if there are symptoms of post-traumatic stress disorder or clinical anxiety.

- Practice being spontaneous or doing things a different way.

- Discover the practice of articulating something good in your life, something concerning you, and something you are hopeful about, sometimes referred to as "rose, thorn, and bud," as a way of doing an in-the-moment self-assessment.

Prayer

Ever-Present and Constant Spirit, help us to embrace pliability and to be comforted by the trust that you are constant, steadfast, and unfailing, even as we sometimes feel like we are drowning in change. As we recognize ways in which our identities and circumstances evolve through life and hardship, please help us stay rooted and strong as we endeavor to be flexible and bendable. Enable us to refrain from judging ourselves and our circumstances as we trust in you and your lovingkindness. Help to calm our anxious spirits, recognizing who and what help us to stay grounded and calm-spirited as we face change and chaos. Free us from the burdens of worry and perfectionism, allowing us to live into each day with a spirit of possibility and hope. Remind us of your promises of love, faithfulness, and allegiance as we journey through life's challenges, and enable us to feel your presence and companionship alongside us. Amen.

4

Problem Solving

A sum can be put right:

but only by going back till you find the error

and working it afresh from that point,

never by simply going on.

—C.S. Lewis[1]

PROBLEM SOLVING IS AN unglamorous but essential component of resilience. Experiencing hardship or trauma almost always leads to unexpected changes in our lives, relationships, or routines. The ways that we were doing things before may no longer work. We may be forced to find new sources of support and new ways of understanding ourselves and the world. To successfully adapt to the "new normal," we must be problem solvers. Problem solving enables us to overcome challenges more effectively and is scientifically associated with increased resilience. In her report entitled "Fostering Resiliency in Kids," social worker Bonnie Benard pointed out that, "Studies on resilient children repeatedly find the presence of problem-solving skills."[2] Some cognitive behavioral therapists have embraced Problem-Solving Therapy as a therapeutic intervention based on this association.

1. Lewis, *Great Divorce*, preface.
2. Benard, "Fostering Resiliency," 4.

Problem-Solving Therapy can be used to help treat depression and anxiety and focuses on "teaching people skills to help them take a more active role in their lives, taking more initiative, and utilizing whatever influence they have to effectively make decisions and achieve their goals."[3] We will be more resilient if we are ready and able to develop our problem-solving skills and use them to live into the new realities that result from our challenges or trauma.

We can find models for successful and creative problem solving in a variety of spiritual, religious, and secular sources. In an ancient Hebrew story, there were two women who lived in the same household, and they bore children at the same time. One of the babies died during the night, and each of the women claimed that the surviving baby was her own. When King Solomon was asked to mediate the dispute, he asked for a sword and said that he would simply cut the child in two, so each could have half. The baby's birth mother quickly spoke up and said, "Please, my lord, give her the living boy; certainly do not kill him!"[4] He knew immediately that this was the birth mother and reunited her with her child. In the Islamic tradition, Muslim scholars are exploring the many ways in which Islamic tradition, the Qur'an, and the testimonies regarding the life of Muhammad, peace be upon him, inform aspects of leadership and management, including problem solving, with one researcher even detailing a problem-solving model based on Islam.[5] In Buddhism, too, problem solving can be done with intentionality and mindfulness through processes such as Analytic Meditation, where "one needs to meditate on the information accumulated by the mind from various sources and use reasoning to decode and decrypt it."[6] Creative problem solving has been valued throughout religious history.

Among examples of spiritually motivated problem solvers are the "Righteous Among the Nations." These were loving, faith-filled people who helped hide, protect, and feed persecuted Jewish men, women, and children during World War II, in spite of the grave risks. Over twenty-two thousand people received this special designation because of their bravery and problem-solving skills. One such story came from the Italian town of Assisi, where around three hundred Jewish individuals were sheltered and protected by Franciscan priest Father Rufino Niccacci. Father Rufino not

3. Cognitive Behavior Therapy Los Angeles, "Problem-Solving Therapy," para. 2.

4. 1 Kgs 3: 8–26 (NRSV).

5. Fontaine, "Problem Solving," 264–74.

6. Dalai Lama, paraphrased in "Dalai Lama on Analytic Meditation," para. 2.

only hid them in monasteries, homes, and convents, but he also helped disguise them and find them employment. He worked closely with the town's printing press, which secretly printed falsified identity cards and documents to ensure their safety.[7] Thanks to Father Rufino's desire to save lives and fight for justice, his ability to identify his resources, and his creative and detailed strategies for implementation, he helped make a difference using his problem-solving skills. There are many other stories throughout history that celebrate creative problem solving. Successful and effective people such as Ruth Bader Ginsburg, Alexander Hamilton, Marie Curie, and Sheryl Sandberg have employed problem-solving skills in order to persevere and flourish in times of adversity.

The military has a long tradition of emphasizing problem solving. I admittedly became weary of being told to maintain a "can-do attitude" during my time in the Coast Guard because it sometimes felt unrealistic and burdensome. The mantra of having a "can-do attitude" translates into this: "The military develops a mindset that failure is not an option. If I am asked to accomplish a mission or a task, I must find a way to get it done. There is no good excuse for failure. There is only an expectation that the mission will be completed."[8] When we needed information or were given a task, we were first required to try to figure it out ourselves using our existing knowledge and resources. If we are unable, we would ask for help from a peer. Only if we exhausted every possible strategy for solving the problem without their help, we were allowed to ask a person senior to us. If that senior person deemed the question unworthy of their answer, it was considered a "bore-ass" question, and we were reprimanded. Needless to say, out of fear and desperation, we learned to be efficient and resourceful, and we honed our problem-solving skills! Although asking for help from my boss was *sometimes* needed, I learned that I could often resolve problems and find answers to questions without needing my supervisor's intervention.

This was one of the greatest gifts the military gave me because problem solving did not come naturally for me. I was fortunate that my parents, teachers, and coaches were incredibly supportive and attentive—my mom even drove me to school every day (which is incredible because I actually lived across the street!)—but I realize now that I didn't have the need or opportunity to solve my own problems until the academy forced me to.

7. *Jewish Virtual Library*, s.v. "Rufino Niccacci," https://www.jewishvirtuallibrary.org/rufino-niccacci.

8. Anderson, "Three Traits," § "Veterans," para. 3.

This punitive system *did* teach me to be determined and creative. Although those of us in the civilian sector do not have to worry about being punished or shamed for asking a "bore-ass" question, we can practice our problem-solving skills by challenging ourselves to solve problems more independently by tapping into our internal and external resources. We may realize that we are better at it than we thought! And if we are not, we will certainly improve with practice.

A key benefit to first looking within ourselves to solve problems is that the solution that is best for us is often unique to us. If I am facing a divorce, for instance, the resolution and arrangement that might work best for me might look very different than that of a friend. If I come to my own resolution that is informed by and not dictated by the advice and information of others, it will likely be a better fit than if I just thoughtlessly do what someone else did or recommended. Sometimes we are inclined to listen to our most vocal friend, succumb to the peer pressure of a coworker, or trust whatever solution is trending on the internet. To embrace a productive and independent problem-solving spirit, we benefit from looking at our problems in practical and realistic ways and following these steps: identify our goals, define the problem, do our research, make a plan, and assess our outcomes.

IDENTIFY OUR GOALS

It is tempting to jump in and want to begin solving problems related to changes we might be experiencing stemming from hardship or trauma, but before solving a problem, and even before defining the problem, it is essential for us to first identify our goals. Using the divorce example, there are varieties of practical and emotional problems and challenges that we need to resolve, such as financial and custody considerations, living arrangements, the grief associated with the divorce, and the anxiety associated with the many impending changes. Before we engage the process of solving these problems and challenges, it is worth articulating our unique goals. Mine possibly would be something like this: to create a full and happy life for myself apart from my partner and to be a role model of grace and forgiveness for my children. Once the goals are articulated, each of the next problem-solving steps should be in service of those goals. When we catch ourselves doing things that are not consistent with these goals, such as sending a passive-aggressive text or venting to the kids, even if it might feel good in the moment, we will benefit from taking time to regroup and reconsider. Being mindful of our goals helps prevent our emotions and instincts from undermining or derailing us.

Identifying our goals allows us to be mindful. Like many newly engaged people (with a Type-A personality), I wanted my wedding day to be as close to perfect as possible. Prior to the big day, I read a variety of books and articles about wedding ceremonies and receptions, learning about the perfect dress, invitations, ceremony elements, and entrées. But one of the simplest and most valuable pieces of advice I discovered was this: decide how you want to behave and feel on your wedding day, and when you realize that you are not behaving that way, make a change. In my case, I made a mindful choice to try to be fun, relaxed, and grateful, and when I caught myself getting snippy with the photographer or obsessing about the bustle on my wedding dress, I was able to recognize the need to adjust my attitude and behavior. This helpful advice is applicable throughout our lives, not just on our wedding days.

Articulating our goals will give us objective benchmarks. It will help us see which of our conversations, emotions, and plans are bringing us closer to our goals and which are working against them. In the example of the divorce situation, we might identify a friend, for instance, who has the capacity to get us angry and riled up and another that helps us feel a greater sense of grace and peace. Spending time with the latter person and being mindful of the emotions stirred up in conversations with the former person will help us move toward reaching the goals we established for ourselves. Identifying our goals gives us focus and intention and enables us to more precisely define the problem we face.

DEFINE THE PROBLEM

Once we identify our goals, we can then work on defining our problems, which is an important step in solving them. We gain power over our problems when we put them into words and use language that is objective and realistic. Engaging in this activity also helps us get to the root. A simple example is this: I may decide that I hate my job and dread going to work. As I think more deeply about it, I can discover what specifically is upsetting me. I reflect on the times I'm feeling frustrated and when I'm feeling fulfilled. I might realize that it is the frantic pace of the job that is making me weary and burned out. Perhaps I can pinpoint which specific tasks are weighing me down and are taking away from the joy related to aspects of the job that I find more important and fulfilling. Perhaps I don't really hate my job, but there may be life-draining parts that I can fix or eliminate using my problem-solving skills. Maybe there are specific tasks that contribute to my sense of franticness that I can reassign, streamline, or eliminate. Defining the problem allows us to focus in on what needs solving and increases our chance of success.

In addition to specifically defining problems, being honest about how we view our problems is important and impactful. In a workshop about resilience designed for attorneys, many of whom are struggling with overwork and burnout, Ann Brafford invited the listeners to see problems as temporary, specific, and external—an optimistic view. In contrast, pessimists see problems as permanent, universal, and internalized.[9] When we face a specific setback or challenge, it does not mean that we are universally inept, incompetent, or hopeless; the challenges we face are often not entirely our own fault and do not reflect our own fundamental character flaws. Sometimes our inner language is extreme—seeing things as exclusively bad, seeing ourselves and our interventions as hopeless, seeing the way in which it is all our fault, and making unhelpful and inaccurate assumptions. Changing our inner language can benefit our ability and enthusiasm for tackling problems that we face, and changing our inner language is a choice. Defining the problem and seeing it as solvable gives us power over it.

Thomas Edison was an example of a bold and committed problem solver who had a gift for defining problems. He was an inventor with over a thousand patents including the incandescent light bulb, and his ability to see what was missing or what was needed drove his innovative spirit. From a very young age, he had a lot going against him and was forced to solve many complex personal and professional problems. Both of his parents had their own challenges that impacted their emotional availability; his dad was in exile in the United States from Canada, and his mother struggled with mental illness. Edison's hearing was severely impaired from childhood illnesses, and he struggled in school with hyperactivity. Fortunately, his inquisitiveness and problem-solving skills led him to read a great deal and to embrace his curiosity, and he courageously took risks and challenged himself.[10] He would look closely and determine what needed to be fixed and

9. Brafford and Knudson, "Building Resilience."

10. *Biography.com*, s.v. "Thomas Edison," https://www.biography.com/people/thomas-edison-9284349.

calculated how best to approach it. This philosophy led to his first patent at age twenty-one and his life as an entrepreneur. He spent his life solving problems and was thought to have said, "I have not failed. I've just found ten thousand ways that won't work."[11]

Like many things, how we frame our problems is habitual. Consistently assuming a negative outcome will inevitably thwart our ability to achieve positive outcomes. We risk creating our own self-fulfilling prophesies, where our negative thinking causes our subconscious to overly focus on the possible negative outcomes and increases their likelihood of coming to fruition. On the other hand, having an optimistic outlook has the opposite effect and opens us to the evidence that disproves what might have been our negative assumptions and generalizations. Being optimistic helps problem solving and increases our likelihood that we will find a solution to the challenges and discover the inner effort and drive needed to persevere. Every problem has a solution, and embracing a "can-do" attitude is essential to resilience. Once we know what exactly the problem is and trust that there's a solution, we can find the energy and enthusiasm to learn more about the problem and possible solutions.

DO THE RESEARCH

The third thing we can do when we approach our problems is to do some research. "If one gives answer before hearing, it is folly and shame," are wise words from the Abrahamic books of wisdom.[12] It is essential we engage in this process of learning with open minds. The solution may not be what we wanted, or it may impact us in certain uncomfortable ways, but our research may show that it is the best solution given the circumstances. The great physicist Albert Einstein was rumored to have said that if he had an hour to solve an important problem, he would spend the vast majority of the time studying it and just a few minutes solving it. As we do our research in preparation for coming up with a plan, we benefit from doing it with an open mind, with a confidence that there is a solution to be discovered, and with an assurance that we are not alone. Our research can involve the valued input of others, the experience of our broader community, and wisdom within ourselves.

11. Exact source unknown, attribution to Thomas Edison is disputed.

12. Prov 18:13 (NRSV).

It is very unlikely that we are the first to be dealing with a certain challenge or crisis, and there are many everyday people and experienced professionals who have wisdom they can share. These individuals can form important networks of support for us as we navigate our challenges. Our first instinct might be to go to social media. While social media can sometimes serve as a resource for crowdsourcing information, it also has some significant liabilities. Instead, reaching out to specific individuals whom we know and trust would likely be most fruitful. Professional support is also a phenomenal way to bolster our support system, and professionals such as therapists, counselors, spiritual directors, or members of clergy have training and expertise that can better help us define our problem and explore solutions. An added bonus is that professionals typically lack the personal investment and bias that our friends and family sometimes bring to the conversations. We can learn a great deal from others.

In addition to individuals, there are support groups and networks that take shape, either in real life or online, that can be lifelines for us when we struggle. When my son Noah was diagnosed with six life-threatening food allergies when he was six months old, I joined online communities dedicated to parents of kids with allergies that were incredibly reassuring, informative, and helpful. Al-Anon is another community of people whose purpose is to "offer the opportunity to learn from the experiences of others who have faced similar problems."[13] Members discuss ways of coping with problems, they share their personal and painful experiences, and they learn strategies for living with someone with a substance abuse problem. Similarly, Alcoholics Anonymous has been around since the thirties and currently supports over two million people who struggle with alcoholism in over 180 countries.[14] Seeking out and using supportive communities is helpful. These communities and the caring people within them provide resources, information, encouragement, and empathy.

A less personal but effective option can be the variety of self-help books available. I admit that I am tempted to change my parenting strategy every few months based on the latest parenting book I've read or most recent article that popped up on social media. There are many comprehensive books that address a variety of challenges and issues. You may not agree with every suggestion that is offered, but our positions mature and grow when we are able to critically assess and either adopt and reject recommendations

13. Al-Anon Family Groups, "How Can I Help," para. 2.
14. General Service Office, "Estimated Worldwide."

or opinions that we read. Since most authors have worked hard to compile and reflect on current research, their advice is generally solidly grounded.

Whether we are young or old, we have valuable life experience that can guide us. We wouldn't be in a position to manage our current challenge if we had not survived a handful of past ones. Reflecting on our own past difficulties and successes can unleash our ability to solve problems in the present moment. We can reflect on things we successfully achieved, and we can identify and celebrate the external resources we accessed, the internal gifts we put into use, and the ways in which we avoided pitfalls and fixed broken things along the way. Similarly, we can reflect on some of our greatest challenges and failures, regardless of whether they resulted from our own errors in judgment, persecution, or just bad fortune. We can look at how we rose above those challenges and assess both the good and bad choices we made while getting through it. We can apply those learnings to what we face today by recognizing the choices and resources that were helpful, as well as those that were not. We can learn equally from our successes and mistakes and can apply those learnings to our current challenge. Connecting with knowledgeable individuals and supportive groups, researching books and articles related to our challenges, and reflecting on our own past achievements and trials can help us prepare a plan.

MAKE A PLAN

After we have identified our goals, defined the problems we need to solve, and done our research, we must take that information and make a plan using short-term and long-term strategies. It is essential that we develop strategies that are in service of our ultimate goals that specifically work toward solving the particular problems we identified. These strategies should be specific, concrete, and measurable.

Brainstorming is a valuable approach and invites us to freely and creatively think of a variety of possible strategies. We can then look at these options and consider the pros and cons of each strategy, identify which strategies are most realistic, and pinpoint which ones are most likely to meet the goals we established in the beginning. Being tactical and intentional avoids trial and error, which saps us of our emotional energy and resources. If we return to the example of an impending separation and divorce, realizing that each of our personal lists would be unique, an example of a set of strategies could look something like this:

- Inventory all financial accounts and assets.

- Research options for mediation or legal action.

- Meet with the attorney to discuss dividing of assets and retirement accounts, child support, and alimony.

- Connect with a divorce support group in town.

- Discuss custody arrangements with my spouse, including the holidays.

- Ask friends if they know a good family therapist in town and make appointments for the kids and myself.

- Set aside time to jog and do yoga.

- Make plans with friends who are understanding and supportive for the weekends or evenings when the kids are with my ex.

- Make a list of the projects and hobbies I want to accomplish when I am home alone.

- Identify groups with which I've been meaning to connect, such as a singing group, adult sports team, or church group.

Creating a list like this helps us break a big problem into smaller ones and enables us to have increased power over our problems and our problem-solving process. Then, take some time to see how things are going.

ASSESS OUR OUTCOMES

As we begin to implement the strategies we established, we can assess how things are going. Assessing our outcomes helps us see how effective our plan was and what we need to do differently. Did we achieve our goals? Were our strategies effective and realistic? Were our original goals the right ones for us? Perhaps we need to create completely new strategies if the strategies we implemented aren't servicing our goals as we intended, or maybe we need to make small adjustments to our strategies or our goals, themselves. Just as Thomas Edison learned from his failures and modified his inventions to meet the goals he identified, we need to be assessing and modifying along the way. When things do not go as planned, we should not consider it a failure, but use it as a learning experience to develop new strategies. Problem solving is a process, and being intentional about engaging in the process with enthusiasm and trust will make us more resilient.

"STRUCK DOWN, BUT NOT DESTROYED"

Meredith describes herself as fun, quirky, intense, and out-spoken. She is fiercely loyal, generous, protective, encouraging, strong, and forgiving. I loved her the moment I met her during our first summer at the Coast Guard Academy. She has a free spirit and unmatched bravery that allows her to live fully into each day and to avoid the trap of taking anything more seriously than it deserves. Meredith was able to make us laugh even when we were feeling overwhelmed and anxious, and she was able to see the good in each one of us. She made me feel loved and appreciated in a context full of judgment and competition, whether on the obstacle course, in the dining hall, or on the volleyball court. We envied her bravado and her healthy perspective. It wasn't until later that I would learn about the life experiences that made her so strong and wise.

Meredith and her brother were raised in DC, and later Maryland, by high-achieving, brilliant, and successful parents. Her early childhood was fairly typical, with sibling shenanigans and frequent trips to the library. One night when she was eleven years old, she awoke to yelling and a hazy room. She got up and walked to the hallway to find it full of smoke. She attempted to make her way down the stairs but was stopped by the heat and smoke of a house fire. She backtracked, grabbed a pillow that she held to her mouth and nose, and she cautiously made her way to her brother's room because she remembered the overhang below the window that enabled her and her brother to jump out onto the front lawn, which they did periodically while playing together. Her brother and mother were out on the ledge, and in a chaotic moment, she remembers feeling her father's hands on her back, firmly guiding her out the window to safety. She, her mother, and her brother were out on the ledge, but her father did not immediately emerge. Although nobody knows exactly what happened or why, her father was later found in the den. He did not survive the fire.

Meredith's grief was crushing. Her father understood her. He loved her deeply and generously made her needs a priority. She lost him, as well as her sense of security, all of her belongings, and the home she knew and loved. Understandably, she struggled to cope with her pain and grief and put up defensive walls. As a result, she found herself in an inpatient psychiatric facility where she spent weeks trying to discover some emotional healing. Even as a young girl, she was forced to hone her problem-solving skills, and she emerged from that terrifying and painful experience as the strong, feisty, and funny (sometimes sarcastic!) woman she is today. Those incredible characteristics, sadly, were not an entirely good fit for the Coast Guard Academy of the early 1990s.

As a cadet at the academy, these characteristics earned her a reputation for being irreverent, which some of the upperclassmen determined was a fatal flaw. These upperclassmen were determined to run her out of the academy and were successful in doing so after their strategic and systematic efforts, scrutinizing her behavior and issuing punishments relentlessly for the most trivial of infractions. Meredith's departure left a huge hole in our hearts and in the Class of 1996, but she again used her problem-solving skills to live into Plan B and joined the enlisted ranks in the Coast Guard, where she was able to fulfill her goals of serving her country, being self-sufficient and independent, and engaging in the important missions of the Coast Guard. Her strong spirit was valued and appreciated, and she became a dear friend and mentor to many of her Coast Guard colleagues. Her life then took another unexpected turn when she became pregnant.

The quick and simple choice might have been to terminate the pregnancy, but Meredith decided to do some research and explore her options. After meeting with a knowledgeable social worker at Catholic Charities named Jean, Meredith decided to engage in an open adoption and gave birth to a daughter named Emma. Emma's adoptive family has become like family to Meredith, and Emma's life has been a blessing to Meredith, providing her with a sense of joy, hope, and gratitude. When time came for Meredith to transition out of the Coast Guard, she became a server at a restaurant in Maryland, again demonstrating her willingness and ability to solve problems and do what she needed to do to be independent and self-sufficient.

The restaurant industry also appreciated her sense of humor, incredible work ethic, and problem-solving skills. She set very explicit goals for herself and measured her success each month, and she systematically checked off the boxes required for promotion in the industry. She moved up quickly to manager and ultimately to her current role as restaurant proprietor. She develops meaningful relationships with her employees and serves as a wise mentor and empathetic mother-figure. It takes an incredibly capable problem solver to successfully run a restaurant, and this has given Meredith the opportunity to continue to develop this important resilience characteristic.

Meredith's resilience was put to the test yet again when she received the call that her best friend since childhood died by suicide. Brie was a successful and loving person, and this devastating news caused Meredith to revisit her childhood grief and question herself. Meredith knew she needed some time to process Brie's death and took over a year off of work to process her grief, while she provided emotional support to Brie's mom and honed her ability to empathetically sit with people in their pain. After one meeting with Brie's mom, Meredith discovered an envelope in her purse. In it was money with a note that said, "I know Brie would want you to finish your college degree. Please use this." In honor of Brie and to fulfill one of her own personal goals, Meredith graduated from college in her forties. She is now exploring ways to continue helping people and serving others and is applying to law school.

Meredith's journey was extremely painful at times, but with wisdom and patience, she has taken life one day at a time, successfully and tenaciously identifying her goals, defining the problems she encountered, doing her research, making plans, and reflecting on outcomes to plan her next steps. She recognizes the relationship between change and problem solving, and she has lived into change with creativity and determination, using her problem-solving skills. She maintains an incredibly healthy attitude about challenges and works to recognize the good that comes from the difficulties she has experienced, realizing that we are each the people we are today because of the lives we have lived, the suffering we have endured, and the joys we have known. Meredith's resilience is captured in this quote from the apostle Paul: "We are afflicted in every way, but not crushed; perplexed, but not driven to despair; persecuted, but not forsaken; struck down, but not destroyed."[15] Meredith truly is a resilient healer who will continue to bless the world with her wisdom, insight, empathy, and love, while she gently but firmly places her encouraging hands on the backs of others as she guides them to safety and helps them grow and succeed.

FINAL THOUGHTS ON PROBLEM SOLVING

Trauma and hardship create changes that require us to make adjustments and find solutions. The solutions are not often obvious or easy or linear, but we will be more resilient when we become better problem solvers. When we cultivate our problem-solving skills as we manage small setbacks and hiccups, problem solving will come more naturally when we face significant challenges and hardships. Although this can be trying when we are in the midst of hardship, let's be inspired by this old saying: "A pessimist sees the difficulty in every opportunity; an optimist sees the opportunity in

15. 2 Cor 4:8–9 (NRSV).

every difficulty."[16] We *can* and *will* become more capable problem solvers by practicing and intentionally employing our problem-solving skills while maintaining a spirit of hope and determination.

REFLECTION AND ACTION

Questions to ponder

- What has been effective for you when solving problems in the past?

- What resources, skills, and gifts do you have that have helped solve problems?

- What can you do to be aware of the times when you imagine the worst or worry about things that have not happened? How can you redirect your thinking?

- How does worry interfere with your life and ability to solve problems? What can help you release or set aside feelings of worry, such as a mantra, prayer, meditation, or deep breathing?

- How can you practice becoming a more systematic person who is able to create and follow steps?

- After you have solved a problem, what strategies can you use to reflect on what went smoothly and what aspects of the problem solving posed challenges for you?

Strategies for cultivating this characteristic of resilience

- Identify and articulate your goals. What are your priorities, values, and hopes for yourself, and how are they reflected in these goals? How are your priorities, values, and hopes also reflected in the short- and long-term strategies you intend to implement?

- Journal about significant accomplishments and cite what problem-solving skills and resources—internal and external—you employed.

- Journal about a problem you encountered in the past and what strategies you used to solve it. Remind yourself of your abilities by looking

16. Source unknown, sometimes attributed (perhaps falsely) to Winston Churchill.

in the mirror and saying this, "My name is _____, and I have bounced back from _____. I can do this!"[17]

- Consider the crisis or problem you may be managing right now and create a step-by-step list of things you can do to work toward solving the problem using these steps: identify your goals, define the problem, do the research, make a plan, and assess your outcomes.

- Identify minor challenges in your life and engage in the five-step problem-solving process to help make problem solving a natural, intentional, and practiced habit.

- Meet with a mentor or counselor to discuss your problems.

- Familiarize yourself with local resources and libraries to enable your research.

- As you solve problems, be intentional about reflecting on what went well and what was difficult, and consider ways that you might do things differently or more effectively next time.

Prayer

Source of Wisdom, help us to recognize our goals—our deepest wishes for ourselves, our families, and communities. Enable us to identify those goals, define our problems, create and implement plans, and assess our outcomes, so that we might achieve these goals that will improve our lives and world. Please place in our paths people, information, and inspiration that enable us to move forward with increased wisdom and effectiveness. Please prevent us from being thwarted by hopelessness or frustration, despair or exhaustion. Enliven our spirits with a "can-do" attitude that can help us break problems down and tackle them with energy, ability, and confidence. When our strategies fail us, imbue us with creative spirits to identify new strategies that will be more effective and help us to not blame ourselves or doubt ourselves when things don't go as planned. Assure us that all problems have solutions, and give us the wisdom and ability to make problem solving a habit. Amen.

---

17. Adapted from Nishioka and Robinson, "Resilience and Joy."

5

Purpose

When you do things from your soul,
you feel a river moving in you, a joy.

—Rumi[1]

THE PRINCIPLES, PEOPLE, BELIEFS, and causes that fill our hearts with passion and conviction constitute our *Purpose*. The strength and determination we gain by identifying and cultivating our sense of purpose enable us to withstand incredible pain, endure adversity, and be positively transformed by hardship or trauma. Arizona's longtime senator John McCain said this: "Nothing in life is more liberating than to fight for a cause larger than yourself, something that encompasses you but is not defined by your existence alone."[2] McCain embodied resilience that seemed driven by his deep sense of purpose that was rooted in his identity and beliefs as an American, as a Christian, and as a leader. This purpose gave him the courage to survive his imprisonment and torture as a prisoner of war during the Vietnam War and to stand up against policies he deemed unjust. While suffering as a prisoner in a notoriously cruel prison camp, McCain demonstrated his commitment to his purpose, and he refused the offer of release until his fellow prisoners were also set free. Meanwhile, he diligently memorized the names of the

1. Rumi, *Soul of Rumi*, 33.
2. McCain, *Faith of My Fathers*, 348.

335 other American prisoners while he was in solitary confinement.[3] He is considered a hero and a maverick for his unwavering faithfulness to his principles and moral beliefs. Like John McCain, our sense of meaning or purpose will empower us to be more resilient and withstand suffering.

People have long recognized the power of purpose, also referred to as one's meaning of life. An entire field of study called logotherapy focuses on finding meaning and "affirm[s] the dignity, freedom, and responsibility of human beings in whatever circumstances they find themselves."[4] It was developed by Austrian psychiatrist Victor Frankl, an incredibly resilient individual who survived Nazi concentration camps and the deaths of nearly everyone in his family, including his pregnant wife. Frankl's suffering caused him to recognize the important role that meaning plays in survival, and he spent much of his life after his release helping others discover meaning in life. He acknowledged that every scenario we face is, as one scholar described it, "an opportunity to act in a meaningful way."[5] In his book *A Man's Search for Meaning*, Frankl said this:

> To be sure, man's search for meaning may arouse inner tension rather than inner equilibrium. However, precisely such tension is an indispensable prerequisite of mental health. There is nothing in the world, I venture to say, that would so effectively help one to survive even the worst conditions as the knowledge that there is a meaning in one's life.[6]

Having meaning is an essential key for survival, and this sense of purpose can be found in even the most dismal circumstances, even if our purpose is simply to bear the suffering with whatever strength and grace we can muster. As we discover what helps us feel enlivened, even when things around us seem desperate, dismal, and lonely, we *can* and *will* find the motivation we need to continue to move forward. We will be more resilient.

Purpose makes us more resilient and makes life worth living, but our purpose is not static or stagnant. We are constantly growing personally, emotionally, and spiritually as we live through difficult situations, expose ourselves to the experiences of others, and befriend and love people different than us. We consciously or unconsciously register the feelings of joy, engagement, and fulfillment that we experience as we interact with the world.

3. McCain, "John McCain," § "Communications," para. 5.

4. Das, "Frankl," 199.

5. Ibid.

6. Frankl, *Man's Search*, 103–4.

These feelings help us discern our sense of purpose—what we are meant to do and where we are meant to serve at any given time. As we go through life, the specific ways in which our purpose manifests may change, and it is also possible that our sense of purpose, itself, may evolve. Developing a sense of purpose is not a singular event but is a life-time endeavor.

One of my colleagues in ministry has been attuned to the evolution of his sense of purpose. Bob began his career in the footsteps of his ancestors. His Grandma Hilda was the first woman ordained in the state of Maine in the mid-twenties and became a seminary professor, and his father was a parish minister in New England. Bob pursued ministry and served as a pastor of small congregations in Maine. His career then took what seemed like an unexpected turn when he transitioned to boat building, and he and his late wife established an organization that created boat-building apprenticeships for people who were struggling to find "a new direction," including those recovering from alcohol or drug addiction, transitioning from prison, or discerning a new vocation after college or at retirement.[7] His sense of call evolved again when he felt led to college ministry. Bob was aware of his gifts and passions and was open to using them to provide support to others, to discover a sense of fulfillment within himself, and to make the world a better place. Even as Bob's specific employment changed, there were key themes within each of his areas of service that brought him joy and fulfillment. In Bob's case, his purpose has been to journey with and to support people in transition. He was constantly open to the dynamic ways his sense of purpose was unfolding. We too would benefit from being open to the evolving nature of our purpose.

Finding meaning and purpose can seem increasingly difficult in a world full of cynicism, insincerity, and hopelessness. Forty-nine of the fifty states in the United States saw a rise in suicide rates,[8] and people who died by suicide span a wide array of demographics, from famous celebrities to young tweens. Developing a sense of purpose is not just a luxurious exercise for the privileged; instead, it is a potentially life-saving necessity. Thankfully, research shows that the millennials and Generation Z are motivated by "purpose, passion, and impact,"[9] and young adults are recognizing the value of discovering and cultivating a sense of purpose. German philosopher Friedrich Nietzsche faced setbacks and loneliness in his life and said,

7. Goldfine, "Bowdoin," para. 3.

8. "Suicide Rates," para. 1.

9. Mercurio, "Meet Generation Z," para. 3.

"If a man knows the wherefore of his existence, then the manner of it can take care of itself."[10] We can all begin this important and fulfilling journey from hopelessness to purpose by mindfully doing the following: exploring our identities, honoring our experiences, defining our beliefs, discerning what brings us joy, assessing our gifts and skills, and having an open mind.

EXPLORING OUR IDENTITIES

Our sense of purpose is ultimately a reflection of who we are as individuals. Our purpose is cultivated in our own unique context and is related to our individual situations, gifts, and experience. Even our woundedness contributes to our sense of purpose in essential ways by giving us deep levels of empathy, compassion, and intuition. I once conducted training for hospice volunteers who were preparing to companion people who were dying. I shared practical information about active listening, the dying process, grief, and self-care. These volunteers were incredibly committed to their work, eagerly absorbed the content, and asked great questions. They also happened to be inmates at a men's prison and were being trained to serve fellow inmates who were dying without access to their families, support systems, and traditional sources of spiritual strength. Because of their own life events and their personal experiences with the criminal justice system, these volunteers were overflowing with compassion as a result of their familiarity with feelings of deprivation, regret, and disconnection. Similarly, sponsors in Alcoholics Anonymous are uniquely equipped to journey alongside people who are working on sobriety and often do so with a commitment and competence that is only possible because of their own journeys. Our struggles, skills, imperfections, gifts, and wounds contribute to our desire and capacity to discover and live into our sense of purpose with vigor and clarity.

The concept of identity is complex, and in addition to our individual identity, we also possess "collective identity," which is described here:

> Collective identity describes imagined as well as concrete communities, involves an act of perception and construction as well as the discovery of preexisting bonds, interests, and boundaries. It is fluid and relational, emerging out of interactions with a number of different audiences.[11]

10. Nietzsche, *Twilight of the Idols*, 2.
11. Polletta and Jasper, "Collective Identity," 298.

Our collective identities impact our sense of purpose because we are mindful of things we need to collectively survive and thrive. We are also able to recognize the injustices and inequities that affect our communities. An example of purpose rooted in collective identity was revealed on what is now called the "Night of Terror" in 1917. Thirty-three members of the National Women's Party women were arrested, physically abused, and held in inhumane conditions because they had been petitioning for voting rights outside of the White House.[12] Their identity as women motivated their sense of purpose which empowered them to risk alienation, arrest, mistreatment, and persecution. We can see the conviction and purpose in this quote from Lucy Stone, one of the original women activists who helped inspire the energy and courage that was demonstrated by the women advocates that horrifying night:

> The last half century has gained for women the right to the highest education and entrance to all professions and occupations, or nearly all . . . By what toil and fatigue and patience and strife and the beautiful law of growth has all this been wrought? These things have not come of themselves. They could not have occurred except as the great movement for women has brought them out and about.[13]

Stone recognized the ability of purpose to empower people to persevere. Our complex and overlapping identities can become the sources of our purpose and can inspire us, just as it motivated many heroines and heroes of the present and past.

HONORING OUR EXPERIENCES

We can also discover a sense of purpose from our personal experiences. Each of our experiences—large and small, profound or mundane, positive or negative—affects our worldviews and passions, and connecting with causes and people related to our experiences can provide a powerful sense of purpose. We can discover a sense of conviction from many things, such as a roommate we meet while hospitalized, a child we encounter on a service trip, or a moving and influential story we hear on public radio. Sadly, our sense of purpose sometimes comes from experiences involving pain

12. McArdle, "Night of Terror," paras. 1–4.
13. Stone, "Progress," final para.

and trauma. Gymnast Rachel Denhollander, for example, is an exceptional athlete who has become a source of comfort and inspiration for survivors of abuse. Among the many victims of sexual abuse at the hands of the team physician, Denhollander was the first to speak out and share heart-felt and personal testimony about the physician's abuse.[14] She was instrumental in bringing the abuser to justice, and as a lawyer, mother, and passionate advocate, Denhollander has become an inspiration for many other women and girls.

I discovered other examples of people with a strong sense of purpose while volunteering at a gun violence prevention conference several years ago. Hanging on a wall behind a table of advocates was a beautiful quilt that was lovingly stitched with bright, happy patterns interspersed with glowing, smiling pictures of young people. These advocates were part of Moms Demand Action and were displaying a sample of the Mother's Dream Quilt Project, a visual representation of the impact of gun violence on communities. The shining and hope-filled faces pictured in the quilt belonged to victims of fatal gun violence who were the children of these advocates. These mothers, along with Hartford-based Mothers United Against Violence and others, dedicate their time and resources to educate, advocate, and influence communities and political leaders. Their sense of shared purpose grew out of their common suffering over losing children to gun violence, and they find meaning in life through this important work they do to prevent others from experiencing the same grief.

The power of the wisdom we gain from our woundedness resulting from painful experiences cannot be understated, and this is a powerful motivator for our purpose. When Marsha Linehan was a teenager, she was hospitalized for over two years because she had suicidal ideations and was diagnosed with schizophrenia. She was reportedly burning herself with cigarettes, cutting, and banging her head against the wall and floor. After working through that deeply dark time, she went on to graduate from college with honors, become a professor of psychology and published author, develop an effective branch of psychotherapy called Dialectical Behavior Therapy, and serve as an empathetic and caring clinical practitioner counseling individuals with complicated and severe mental health challenges.[15] Linehan's story could have ended with a life of institutionalization or suicide, but she instead used her wisdom and life experience to motivate her

14. "Read Rachael," para. 1.
15. Carey, "Expert on Mental Illness," § "I Was in Hell."

sense of purpose, which has had a profound impact on many. All of these examples show how our experiences can motivate our sense of purpose. That which was harmful and painful can enable us become passionate advocates and world-changers.

DEFINING OUR BELIEFS

Our philosophies and worldviews—our belief systems, in other words—are a significant part of who we are and have a major effect on how we interact with the world. When we take time to identify, articulate, and celebrate these beliefs, they can also serve as sources of our sense of purpose. These belief systems are products of a variety of influences, most notably our families, our spiritual or religious traditions, and our political ideologies.

From an early age, we learn values and priorities from our families of origin and from adult role models. We enthusiastically accept and internalize some of these values and priorities, while others may choose *not* to share or emulate. For instance, our families of origin may inspire a passion in us to care for children, veterans, or older adults. They may motivate us to advocate for the environment, education, or women's rights. They can instill in us enthusiasm to serve in civil or military service. The beliefs we internalize from our families of origin help shape our sense of purpose as an adult.

Similarly, our religious or spiritual beliefs can be a foundation of our sense of purpose. Some who identify as religious believe our purpose comes from the Divine, such as author Rick Warren, whose book *The Purpose Driven Life* has sold over thirty-two million copies. In the opening part of the book, Warren says this:

> The purpose of your life is far greater than your own personal fulfillment, your peace of mind, or even your happiness. It's far greater than your family, your career, or even your wildest dreams and ambitions. If you want to know why you were placed on this planet, you must begin with God. You were born by his purpose and for his purpose. [16]

For many people of faith, discernment of purpose is done reflectively and prayerfully, believing that our purpose is from a divine source or higher power. Reformed Christian theologian John Calvin believed that one must

---

16. Warren, *Purpose Driven Life*, 21.

fulfill God's calling in order to be truly faithful, and that calling is our purpose in life. Calvin said, "Every individual's line of life, therefore, is, as it were, a post assigned him by the Lord, that he may not wander about in uncertainty all his days."[17] Our spiritual or religious beliefs can help mold our sense of purpose, give us direction, and inspire us to be faithful to that purpose.

For those with a spiritual framework that is not centered around a higher power, purpose can be derived from spiritual beliefs that are not inherently religious, such as the Golden Rule—the responsibility to treat others as we would want to be treated. Embracing the values of equality and compassion and developing purpose around them can be life-giving and sustaining. Rabbi Harold Kushner, author of *When All You've Ever Wanted Isn't Enough: The Search for a Life That Matters*, said this:

> Our souls are not hungry for fame, comfort, wealth, or power . . . Our souls are hungry for meaning, for the sense that we have figured out how to live so that our lives matter, so that the world will be at least a little bit different for our having passed through it.[18]

Our sense of purpose can be a deep comfort and powerful motivation when we are suffering. It helps move us forward, even when we are feeling defeated and hopeless.

Our political ideologies can be yet another source of inspiration as we define our sense of purpose. An inspiring example of this is a leader I mentioned earlier, Nelson Mandela, referred to as the "father of South Africa's democracy."[19] His strength and resilience was evident in his co-creation of the first black law firm in Johannesburg and in his tireless political advocacy for racial equality, which included an epic thirty-year imprisonment. He said, "The struggle is my life," and his obituary said, "It was also through Mandela that the world would learn the spirit of endurance, the triumph of forgiveness and the beauty of reconciliation."[20] President Mandela's deep sense of purpose enabled him to endure and focus on a greater meaning instead of the pain and disappointment near at hand. Like Nelson Mandela, we can potentially withstand unimaginable circumstances and find deep

---

17. Calvin, quoted in "Calvin on Vocation," para. 3.
18. Kushner, *When All You've Ever Wanted*, 18.
19. "Obituary: Nelson Rolihlahla Mandela," para. 1.
20. Ibid., para. 5.

inner strength, forgiveness, and bravery if we identify and embrace a sense of purpose rooted in our beliefs.

DISCERNING WHAT BRINGS US JOY

Another strategy for determining and pursuing our purpose is identifying the activities, subjects, and people that make our hearts joyful and our spirits fulfilled. The word "joy" can be misleading; I doubt John McCain was "joyful" about suffering in solidarity with his fellow prisoners of war, but I imagine that pursuing his purpose by adhering to his moral beliefs and honoring his country gave him a sense of deep satisfaction in knowing he was doing the right thing—doing what his conscience, or God, or his values were calling him to do. The joy discovered by engaging in our purpose is not the same as self-indulgent pleasure or hedonism. The differences between "hedonic well-being" and the well-being associated with meaning and purpose, known as "eudaimonic well-being," are substantial; while the prior indulges you in the moment, the latter relates to the deep satisfaction we find in "fulfilling our potential and feeling that we are part of something bigger than ourselves."[21] The joy associated with purpose relates to a sense of fulfillment stemming from the knowledge that our gifts, skills, and interests are being put to good use and that we are making a difference.

As we go through life, we discover times when we feel deep joy. Being attuned to this joy enables us to discover what gives us satisfaction, fulfillment, inspiration, and renewal. Whether it is caring for grandkids or aging parents, volunteering for an advocacy group, discovering a fulfilling hobby or talent, or engaging new cultures and places through traveling, there are activities that have the capacity to bring us joy and help us feel alive. Therapist Paul Wong developed a type of psychotherapy focused around making meaning that grew out of Victor Frankl's logotherapy, and he stated, "Most of us know intuitively that we experience the deepest satisfaction when we engage in meaningful activities and we feel fully alive, when we passionately pursue a worthy life goal."[22]

As I was considering my own sense of purpose, I discovered joy and felt "fully alive" providing emotional and spiritual support to individuals in a prison, psychiatric hospital, military, hospice, and college. For years I thought I was just vocationally indecisive because these contexts seemed

21. Grenville-Cleave, *Positive Psychology*, 8–9.
22. Wong, "Meaning Therapy," 154.

so different, but I realized that there was a common thread among these diverse contexts. I loved meeting with people one-on-one and exploring with them what it means to be loved by the Divine, to be created with uniqueness, to have special gifts, to be precious and valuable, to be human, and to connect deeply with the universe and with others. I discovered my purpose—to serve people in marginalized or misunderstood populations. I came to recognize the ways in which my own history of marginalization and loneliness informs, inspires, sustains, and benefits my work. Presbyterian minister Frederick Buechner said it well: "The place God calls you to is the place where your deep gladness and the world's deep hunger meet."[23] When we identify activities and causes that bring us joy and make us feel alive, we discover our calling—our purpose.

ASSESSING OUR GIFTS AND SKILLS

Each of us has a unique set of gifts and skills that helps define our potential. Our unique gifts and skills likely align with activities, initiatives, or vocations that could serve to fulfill our sense of purpose. As a child, I absolutely loved volunteering at our local nursing home and had hundreds of hours of service. I was so excited the day my sister Megan agreed to come with me. We arrived together and went off in different directions until we were reunited at the end of the day. As we were heading home, we shared about our days. My sister told me the story of a wheelchair-bound patient who asked my sister to bring her to her third floor room. My sister tirelessly wheeled her all over the hospital trying to locate an elevator before realizing the hospital was only one level. My big-hearted sister confessed that the day was challenging and emotionally draining for her, and she didn't like it one bit! Meanwhile, Megan was incredible with children and was the most popular neighborhood babysitter. The neighbors apparently noticed my dislike for babysitting and my lack of aptitude for it because they would only settle for me as their babysitter if my sister were busy! What won't come as a surprise is that my sister's talents and her love of working with children have only grown, and she is now serving as a high school principal, while I have found deep fulfillment working as a chaplain to older adults. Even from young ages, we each recognized what activities brought us joy, and we identified our individual gifts, passions, and skills that either aligned or misaligned with our activities.

23. Buechner, *Wishful Thinking*, 119.

Some people of faith believe that our talents and skills are gifts given by the Divine. In the Christian New Testament, the apostle Paul writes this:

> We have gifts that differ according to the grace given to us: prophecy, in proportion to faith; ministry, in ministering; the teacher, in teaching; the exhorter, in exhortation; the giver, in generosity; the leader, in diligence; the compassionate, in cheerfulness.[24]

For those who believe that God is the source of our talents and skills, the fact that our talents and skills would align with our purpose would be a sensible conclusion. God gives us skills and talents to enable us to fulfill the purpose that God is putting on our hearts. Whether we believe God is the origin of our talents and skills or not, recognizing our areas of giftedness could help us define our sense of purpose.

HAVING AN OPEN MIND

Finally, having an open mind is essential to finding our purpose. It requires humbleness and flexibility, and it puts us in the position to discover what truly gives us meaning. Without an open mind, we might be closed off to the possibilities of purpose or lack the inclination to pursue it. We can work on having an open mind about our sense of purpose by being open to coincidence and by being willing to go outside our comfort zones.

Our sense of purpose is often discovered in unlikely or coincidental situations. As a theist—someone who believes in God—I attribute coincidences, or synchronicity, to divine inspiration or influence, though others might see it as fate or simply as just that—coincidence. The Hebrew Bible says, "The human mind may devise many plans, but it is the purpose of the Lord that will be established."[25] Buddhism and Hinduism also acknowledge the role of synchronism, which inspired scholars like Carl Jung, the founder of analytical psychology, to explore the role of synchronism in counseling and psychotherapy.[26] In one article, scholars emphasize the importance of recognizing the relevance of synchronicity in career counseling and state, "Therapeutic techniques common to Jungian analysis, such as meditation, guided imagery, active imagination, and dream analysis, can provide a rich environment that may stimulate recognition of 'coincidences' as indicators

---

24. Rom 12:6–8 (NRSV).

25. Prov 19:21 (NRSV).

26. Guindon and Hannah, "Coincidence," 198–99.

of significant career directions."[27] Coincidences can help point us in the right direction or connect us with people who can lead us to lives that have a deeper sense of meaning. Coincidences will present themselves in our lives, so let's be open to them. As we engage in discernment of our purpose, we benefit from doing it with openness, which sometimes leads us right out of our comfort zones.

We are unlikely to truly discover our sense of purpose if we are not open to going outside our comfort zones. My first day as a hospital chaplain as a fledgling seminary student was going smoothly until my on-call beeper sounded midway through the morning. A patient died, and I was asked to provide support to the family and say a prayer at the bedside. I had never seen a dead body outside a funeral home, and I felt crippled with anxiety. I breathlessly asked the Catholic sister who was in the office to come with me, but she knew the protocol. She calmly said, "Nope, you have to go alone. You'll be fine." I doubted my weak legs would get me to the room, but I somehow showed up at the unit. I visited with the kind-hearted and grieving family, learned about the man's wonderful and full life, and said a prayer at the bedside of the deceased. I departed with a joy-filled heart and knew I had found my purpose. When we are open to going outside of our comfort zone—out of a predictable and consistent job, into a new country, to the Women's March in DC, into an art class or college course, to a road race to raise funds for a good cause, out of an unhealthy relationship—we give ourselves the opportunity to find joy and fulfillment and *purpose*.

"LOOK AT THE BIG PICTURE"

For Laurie, she learned early about focus and achieving goals. From a young age, her dad ingrained in her this philosophy: you can do anything you want, as long as you set your mind to it and make it a high enough priority. It gave Laurie determination and motivation that enabled her to achieve incredible things. To be honest, when I first met her at the academy, she was intimidating. She was tough on herself and had high expectations of others. She was rigorous in her attention to detail, adherence to rules and regulations, and dedication to her academic achievement. She was gifted in music and worked hard to meet the physical fitness requirements. She rarely let down her guard and had an unflappable stoic and professional

27. Ibid., 206.

disposition. She was a model cadet and moved up the ranks to regimental executive officer, the second-highest-ranking student in the corps of cadets.

Over time, I came to better understand and value her story and the bumpy path that led her to the Coast Guard Academy. When she was in high school, she had a goal to study oceanography in college and spend a life at sea. She had to be self-sufficient and worked three jobs over the summer to earn money. Because she was without a vehicle, she rode her bike to these jobs so she wouldn't miss a paycheck. She diligently researched her options to attend the Naval Academy or receive a scholarship through the Reserve Officer Training Corps, commonly known as ROTC. Though the Naval Academy was her first choice, she was initially rejected and attended Iowa State University for a year using a Navy ROTC scholarship. She was determined to make her dream of studying the ocean and going to sea a reality, so she built up her transcript and references and applied again to both the Naval and Coast Guard Academies. She was offered appointments at both, and chose to attend the latter.

So when she arrived at the Coast Guard Academy, she wasn't giggly with immaturity or distracted by drinking or dating. She was focused on her goals and allowed her choices to be driven by her sense of purpose with a maturity beyond her years. Since then, she spent many years at sea on Coast Guard ships, attended law school, and dedicated over twenty years to active duty service while raising a child—my Godson. She has learned to be gentler with herself and others, and she has come to appreciate that even with an intense and important purpose and indefatigable energy, it is okay to sometimes fall short. She was even able to laugh at herself when she fell overboard during a law enforcement boarding on the first day as the executive officer (the second most senior person on board) of a Coast Guard vessel. The ship's captain quipped as part of an update on the loud speaker, "The executive officer really did get her feet wet today!"

As a commissioned officer on ships of several sizes deploying for various lengths of time, Laurie was instrumental in helping the Coast Guard execute its essential duties, including law enforcement, search and rescue, and maritime safety. She loved being at sea, serving her country, and being a part of a community of hard-working service members, in spite of the around-the-clock responsibilities, danger, rough seas, and minimal communications with those at home. As she reflected on her love of being at sea, she came to realize that one of the things she loved most was the ability to ease others' burdens. At sea, she discovered what drove her—her *purpose*—to make a difference by having a positive impact. Being a leader in the Coast Guard gave her the opportunity to do that in very tangible and rewarding ways, such as in mentoring junior officers and crewmembers, enforcing the laws that help protect our country, and engaging in maritime safety operations and rescues. Her commitment to making a difference helped her persevere day by day, in spite of the physical and emotional demands of seagoing life.

Going to sea on military deployment is disruptive and challenging, but her situation became more difficult when she left behind her toddler during her deployments, which ranged from six to eight weeks at a time. Although hard, the time away was made easier by her commitment to helping her crew and aiding those who needed the Coast Guard's assistance. She deeply enjoyed her service to the Coast Guard's mission (while the parenting of her very supportive and resilient spouse also helped!), and she stayed focused on her seagoing responsibilities and on her vow to protect and defend the Constitution. It was not easy, but she looked at it this way:

> Having an objective or bigger purpose turns what some might consider to be insurmountable obstacles into challenges to work through, and sometimes the challenges are necessary to help you get to where you want to be. It's like a Cézanne or Monet – you don't see the little brushstrokes (obstacles) when you look at the big picture (goal/mission).

After experiencing sea duty as a parent, Laurie acknowledged that prolonged time away was not working for her family. She recognized where her help was needed most and decided to permanently transition from sea to land as she continued her service as a Coast Guard lawyer. This was a consequential and bitter-sweet choice because of her love of the sea, but she discovered ways to make a difference for people and for our country in her new position and has continued to fulfill her sense of purpose, while also discovering deep joy and fulfillment in being with her family in a more consistent, impactful way.

Laurie's resilience has always been grounded in her sense of purpose rooted in making a difference by having a positive impact. She is grateful for the ways that she has become more aware of this purpose as her life evolved and how this purpose has matured and has sustained her during difficult times. She is dedicated to making a difference and has discovered various ways of doing that during different seasons of her life. To do so, Laurie has overcome substantial obstacles to make her goals realities. She is a remarkable, introspective, and loving woman who is a loyal and compassionate friend. Her focus and dedication is an inspiration to many.

FINAL THOUGHTS ON PURPOSE

As a motivation to define and develop our sense of purpose, let us be mindful of how we want to be remembered. I officiated at many funerals as a hospice chaplain, and one funeral stuck with me. It was a funeral for an older woman, and the only endearing thing the family shared about the deceased was her love of dollar stores. I was somewhat sad for this woman. Suddenly acutely aware of my own love of dollar stores, I thought to myself, "Please, Lord, don't let my only legacy be my love of dollar stores!" In contrast, there is a beautiful memorial at our local rose garden for a woman who is referred to as a sagacious thinker, altruistic visionary, pioneering female lawyer, champion of women's rights, patron of health research, and lover of science.[28] What a tribute! Although I never met this woman, I have a warm feeling for her and am grateful for whatever she did to make the world a better place. Discovering our purpose can motivate us to have a lasting positive impact on other people and on our communities.

It is never too late to discover and redefine ourselves. The fictional Ebenezer Scrooge shows that our futures can be rewritten and marked with the positive, unselfish, and loving things we do in fulfillment of our purpose. It is never too late to become the goofy and loving grandma or one of the older adults participating in the Poor People's Campaign or letter writing project for environmental justice. The famous suffragist Susan B. Anthony spoke of the power and wisdom of age and said, "The older I get, the greater power I seem to have to help the world; I am like a snowball—the further I am rolled the more I gain."[29] As we consider our legacy, we can ask ourselves the question, "When I look back, am I satisfied with the life I have lived?"[30]

Our sense of purpose evolves and changes throughout our lives, and it gives us strength and resolve when we face challenges and difficulties. Purpose helps focus our angst and worry, inspires our effort, and combats fatigue and hopelessness. Although we may sometimes fall short or feel overwhelmed by the extent of need, continually working to identify and

28. Ethel F. Donaghue, memorial, Elizabeth Park, Hartford, CT.

29. Harper, *Life and Work*, 2:859.

30. Grenville-Cleave, *Positive Psychology*, 49.

fulfill our sense of purpose can fuel our energy to continue moving forward. Blogger and author Glennon Doyle said this when talking about the importance of purpose in her life, specifically related to addiction:

> I know that I needed to be invited not only out of addiction, but into a movement to change the world. I needed to join folks working to turn this planet into a gentler, saner, safer, more vivid place in which folks with wide-open eyes and tender hearts might survive and thrive. This is why the moment I stepped out of the world of addiction, I stepped into family, faith, art, service, and activism. I stepped into worlds of purpose.[31]

May we confidently "step out" of the world that is familiar and "step into worlds of purpose."

REFLECTION AND ACTION

Questions to ponder

- What hobbies do you have or could you develop that would bring you deep joy and fulfillment?

- What are you passionate about? What do you find yourself researching, reading about, or discussing?

- What makes you lose track of time or forget to eat?

- What individual or collective identities shape who you are and how you operate in the world? How do they relate to the issues you care about?

- When you have faced difficulties in the past, what goals or convictions have helped you endure?

Strategies for cultivating this characteristic of resilience

- Journal about what in your life gives you meaning and what gifts and skills you possess.

- Ask yourself, "What problem do I want to solve?"

31. Doyle, "Mentally Different," para. 6.

- Create a six-word purpose statement that you would use to identify yourself, such as "Abider in God's faith, hope, and love," and remind yourself of this statement often.[32]

- Look to connect with a therapist who is trained in logotherapy or meaning therapy.

- Be mindful about how different activities make you feel; take note of those activities that give you life and energy.

- Create a spreadsheet that details what you spend your time doing, and as you look at each activity, indicate whether you are spending too much time, just enough time, or not enough time doing it. Make adjustments to your schedule based on those findings, and try to spend as much time as possible on the life-giving, nourishing, and meaningful activities.

- Meet with a spiritual director to explore your passions and calling.

- Get involved in organizations and clubs that are consistent with your passions and beliefs.

Prayer

Spirit of Intention, enable us to identify and cultivate the special gifts and skills you have given us. Help us identify and fuel the passions and convictions you put in our hearts. Make us tools of change to help make the world better, and help us to have a positive impact on our loved ones, neighbors, and communities. Connect us with employment, activities, and hobbies that fill our spirits with fulfillment and peace, and gently correct us when we fall into the temptation of squandering or minimizing our potential. Teach us to take care of ourselves and recognize the activities that renew us. Allow us to be open in mind and spirit to ways in which we can serve others, and please help us overcome our feelings of fear or insecurity that risk holding us back. Regardless of the amount of time we have on earth, help us to make a positive lasting impact and contribute to your kingdom by inspiring us to share your unconditional love and unending patience with others. May we discover and pursue our divinely inspired purpose with humbleness, zeal, and intention, and may it give us strength to grow stronger in hardship. Amen.

32. Nishioka and Robinson, "Resilience and Joy."

6

Piety

Ask, and it will be given you;
search, and you will find;
knock, and the door will be opened for you.
For everyone who asks receives,
and everyone who searches finds,
and for everyone who knocks, the door will be opened.

—MATTHEW 7:7–8 (NRSV)

IT SEEMS THAT ORGANIZED religion is increasingly seen as old-fashioned and obsolete. While three-quarters of adult Americans consider themselves spiritual, far fewer identify as religious.[1] Regardless, we are all spiritual beings with diverse and unique spiritual needs that may relate to belonging, purpose, meaning, morality, or love. So this chapter is for everyone—those who identify as "spiritual but not religious," religious skeptics, the devout, atheists, agnostics, and the unaffiliated. The title of the chapter admittedly may deserve an eye roll, but I honestly couldn't think of any better "P" word than *Piety* to address the wide breath of spiritual or religious communities, practices, and beliefs that help us become more resilient.

---

1. Lipka and Gecewicz, "More Americans," infographic 1.

In nearly every secular, spiritual, and religious tradition, role models of resilience and the encouragement to overcome trauma and struggle are pervasive. Author and psychologist Brené Brown said this in her book *Rising Strong*: "Getting back on our feet does not require religion, theology, or doctrine. However, without exception, the concept of spirituality emerged from the data as a critical component of resilience and overcoming struggle."[2]

For those who have a religious affiliation or identity, connecting with spiritually meaningful communities, practices, and beliefs may be more straightforward. Organized religious groups often have cohesive congregations and regular gatherings, spiritual and religious observances and rituals, comforting theological beliefs that are woven into their histories and identities, and inspirational stories and role models that inspire our faith, trust, and hope. The ways in which faith empowered and sustained German Lutheran pastor and theologian Dietrich Bonhoeffer can serve as an inspiration. He courageously voiced his opposition to Adolf Hitler and the Nazi regime during World War II and was imprisoned. Throughout his writings from prison, he shares intimately about his faith and about the strength and hope it provided him while he was in captivity. His faithfulness and strength of spirit are seen here:

> I believe that God both can and will bring good out of evil. For that purpose he needs men who make the best use of everything. I believe God will give us all the power we need to resist in all time of distress . . . A faith as strong as this should allay all our fears for the future . . . I believe God is not just timeless fate, but that he waits upon and answers sincere prayer and responsible action.[3]

Bonhoeffer found comfort, calm, and patience in a loving, generous, and equipping God that he came to know through his religious tradition. Spirituality or religion can be a grounding emotional support during difficult times.

The benefits of being "religiously involved" are not just anecdotal; the advantages are also supported by science.[4] Those who are religiously involved reportedly enjoy better mental and physical health than their non-religious counterparts, including lower levels of reported pain, lower

---

2. Brown, *Rising Strong*, 10.

3. Bonhoeffer, *Prisoner for God*, 21.

4. This does not apply to affiliation with religious cults and extremism, which negatively affect these conclusions; Koenig, *Is Religion Good*, 101.

risk of stroke, lower blood pressure, and even lower rates of cancer.[5] Those who are spirituality or religiously connected also have fewer hospital stays and shorter hospitalizations.[6] In addition to the positive impacts on health, spirituality and religion can also provide people with a sense of connection, sense of purpose, and hope. Developmental psychologist Emmy Werner said, "A number of studies of resilient children from a wide variety of socio-economic and ethnic backgrounds have noted that their families have held religious beliefs that provided stability and meaning to their lives, especially in times of hardship and adversity."[7] This stability is crucial because when things are going wrong in our lives, having consistency and predictable support can serve as lifelines. In one study, religion was shown to reduce the suicidal ideation of people suffering from depression.[8] In another, those with a "religious orientation" were more likely to have an increased sense of meaning and self-esteem, both of which are crucial elements of resilience.[9] Embracing spirituality or religion benefits our emotional, physical, and mental health, and thus, our resilience.

In spite of those benefits, people are generally becoming less religious. In a *Newsweek* article entitled "The End of Christian America," sociologist Jon Meacham cited a survey that stated that the number of Americans asserting no religious affiliation increased nearly twofold between 1990 and 2009.[10] Sociologist Mark Chavez agrees with this trend and said, "Since the evidence for a decades-long decline in American religiosity is now incontrovertible . . . the burden of proof has shifted to those who want to claim that American religiosity is not declining."[11] There are many things contributing to this reduced religious connection, including the fact that people are marrying later, having fewer children, and working full time.[12] We can be disappointed and regretful about the erosion of this element of resilience, but have hope. With some intention and patience—and even some courage and risk taking—this is an attainable characteristic for us all, regardless of our religious or spiritual history or lack thereof. We can

---

5. Ibid., 103–4 (citing other sources).

6. Southwick, "Promoting Resilience."

7. Werner, quoted in Benard, "Fostering Resiliency," 12.

8. Dervic et al., "Religious Affiliation," § "Discussion," para. 2.

9. Błażek and Besta, "Self-Concept Clarity," 947.

10. Meacham, "End," para. 1.

11. Chavez, "Decline," 9.

12. Wuthnow, *After the Baby Boomers*, 54–66.

cultivate our resilience by focusing on three areas of religious or spiritual strength and connection: community, practices, and beliefs.

SPIRITUAL OR RELIGIOUS COMMUNITY

Various communities in Africa recognize and model the vitality and importance of being connected to supportive and loving communities. The Igbo people of Nigeria, for instance, have a saying, "Gidi gidi bụ ugwu eze," which means, "Unity is strength."[13] One scholar said this:

> Man is not just an individual, an island, left to himself and sufficient to himself, on his own. Man is essentially community. No one ever came to being as a bolt from the blues, like an oil bean seed falling from the sky, as our proverb says, "I am always we."[14]

Those of us in Western culture tend to celebrate and glamorize President Herbert Hoover's concept of "rugged individualism," but, whether by choice or not, we are actually already part of an interconnected web of community that provides our nourishment, healthcare, utilities, public safety, transportation, manufactured goods, and much more. The fictional and popular post-apocalyptic television shows and movies illustrate that none of us would last very long on our own! Embracing our connectedness can be sustaining and essential, and it can provide life-giving material support, emotional support, accountability, and education.

When we think of connecting with a spiritual or religious community, we sometimes think of the cost of membership or the obligation of giving financial support, but I have been on the receiving end of my faith community's generosity more than once. I was already seven months pregnant when we moved to Connecticut in 2007, and my husband and I found a kind congregation that enthusiastically welcomed us. Even though I was new to the church, visits and meals began arriving the day my son was born. In the months and years following, the church helped sustain me with encouragement and support. The "grandmas" of the congregation volunteered to babysit for our children in the church nursery so the Women's Bible study could gather biweekly. This offered a desperately needed break from the relentless job of parenting young children, gave me a place for spiritual growth, and enabled me to develop deep and lasting friendships

13. Chinonye, "Igbo Proverbs," proverb 2.
14. Okere, quoted in Agulanna, "Community and Human Well-Being," 290–91.

with phenomenal women who provided encouragement, advice, and laughs. When one member's husband lost his job, we collected funds for grocery store gift cards. Meals were prepared when another member was undergoing medical treatment. A good spiritual or religious community provides a variety of material benefits, including social events, educational programs, music programs, child care, and sometimes direct financial support. They will be supportive when you need it, and within that supportive and encouraging context, you will be inspired to support the community and others within it in return.

Spiritual or religious communities provide more than just material support. They also provide emotional support and encouragement. Supporting the suffering and the afflicted is a priority of many of these communities, as shown in their prayer lists, memorials, and visitation schedules. Some of my warmest childhood memories include holiday visits with my church to Cobblestone Nursing Home where we would sing Christmas carols and visit facility-bound parishioners. I learned at a young age that everyone has value and deserves love and respect, particularly those whom the culture had forgotten, those with physical or cogitative limitations, and those that seem to be a "drain" on the resources of their towns or families. And as I grew older, I was loved and respected by my Sunday school teachers and received a graduation blessing before leaving for college. In college, I received encouraging notes and care packages, reminding me of my spiritual "home" and my belovedness. In our community of faith, we supported each other and valued each other. Knowing that I was loved, supported, and valued helped me tremendously during the trying years I spent at the Coast Guard Academy and beyond.

In addition to the material and emotional support, a spiritual or religious community can lovingly keep us accountable. In his book *Life Together*, Dietrich Bonhoeffer celebrated the benefit of community to encourage, but also to correct and redirect one another, which he bravely did by voicing his opposition to the ways in which some Christian churches were condoning and enabling Adolf Hitler's rise to power and antisemitism. Reverend Bonhoeffer formed the Confessing Church movement to uphold the religious and spiritual values that church leadership was sidelining, and he held church leaders to account for their complicity. Being in community with one another helps us adhere to ethical and moral values and provides resources to consult when we have questions about choices and priorities. A spiritual or religious community can provide us with common language to discuss issues related to suffering, relationships, generosity, commitment, social justice, and community service. This aspect of community should not seem intrusive or onerous; it instead offers a space for loving accountability, collaboration, and increased self-awareness. I admit that my driving became markedly calmer when I put a Christian bumper sticker on my car, lest my impatience and aggressiveness reflect badly on my community! When we are a part of the community, we want to help the community grow and succeed by upholding the values of the community and by being loving representatives of that community.

Finally, a spiritual or religious community can provide us with knowledge through education. We learn about the history of our traditions and the heroines and heroes who paved the way for us. We can discover spiritual role models and mentors within the community to help us stay connected and focused during difficult times. During such times, we can be strengthened by sermons or khutbahs, studies of our holy writings, and educational programs that expose us to inspiring and relevant belief systems and spiritual practices. As we establish ourselves within the community, we can serve as mentors and teachers, also helping bolster our resilience by increasing our sense of purpose and connection. The importance of the education provided by a spiritual or religious community cannot be understated and is something that people who hesitate to connect with a religious or spiritual community or identify as "unaffiliated" might be missing.

Admittedly, finding a community that is a good fit can be a challenge. My husband and I attended twenty-six different congregations when we moved to the Boston area for graduate school before settling on a congregation that felt socially and theologically comfortable. There were many times I considered giving up, but I knew from my childhood that healthy, loving, welcoming congregations with theological beliefs consistent with my own existed, and I maintained hope that I would find one. Connecting with religious or spiritual communities can provide material support, emotional encouragement, accountability, and education, and these communities can also expose us to nurturing spiritual practices that can help us stay strong and focused.

SPIRITUAL OR RELIGIOUS PRACTICES

Spiritual or religious practices can improve our resilience by enhancing our connection with the Holy or with the universe, more broadly, and by improving our overall emotional centeredness. Attending community gatherings, joining a small group, reading our sacred texts or inspirational writings, participating in the sacraments and rituals, and engaging in contemplative practices like meditation or prayer are examples of activities that can support us during challenging and seemingly hopeless times. Creating habits of spiritual practices gives us a foundation of centeredness that is essential when the storms of life present themselves.

If we identify as religious, there are likely a variety of practices within our traditions that we can do more consistently that can help us feel connected to the Holy, a connection that can be nourishing and assuring. In eighth grade, I was responsible for delivering the sermon for Youth Sunday. With *a lot* of help from my mentor, Jim Dieterle, I preached a sermon entitled "Have You Talked to Your Best Friend Lately?" It spoke about investing in our relationship with God. When we see a friend from high school for the first time at the twenty-year reunion, it is somewhat awkward and intimidating. In contrast, there is a naturalness, intimacy, and authenticity in the conversations with the friend that we've been calling regularly or emailing with consistency. Those mundane conversations throughout the years pave the way for the moments when we are facing hardship or unwanted changes in our lives and need support. It doesn't feel weird to reach out. It makes sense that the same applies to our relationship with God. Even though God would be there for us like a faithful friend whether or not we've been in touch, it feels easier and more comfortable if that relationship with God is one we've been nurturing—if we treat God as a best friend whose relationship we value and prioritize. We can "stay in touch" with God through prayer.

Prayer is an easy, free, and accessible way of connecting more deeply. It can be done anywhere and anytime. While finding reproducible, scientific proof of prayer's efficacy is not easy, many trust in prayer's ability to improve mental and physical health. One researcher addressed the various ways that prayer could be helpful:

> (a) Prayer may improve health because of the placebo effect; (b) individuals who pray may also engage in health-related behaviour; (c) prayer may help by diverting attention from health problems; (d) prayer may promote health through supernatural intervention by God; (e) prayer may activate latent energies, such as chi, which have not been empirically verified, but which nevertheless may be beneficial to health; and (f) prayer may result in a unity

of consciousness which facilitates the transmission of healing between individuals.[15]

Whatever the reason, prayer is worthwhile if it brings comfort and hope,
helps us feel more connected with the Holy, or invites us to recognize and
express gratitude. Prayer is also a way of acknowledging wrongdoing and
asking for forgiveness for ourselves or others, and it allows us to engage in
the important practices of reflection and self-understanding. Prayer need
not be overthought. My former Muslim colleague Sami had prayer beads
with him nearly all the time to use while waiting in line, during a boring
meeting, or even while stuck in traffic. Our prayer could take the form of
a simple sigh, a comforting mantra, thoughts of gratitude, a kind gesture
toward another person, or even our tears. Framing these activities as prayer
can help us be more mindful of our connection with the Holy and with the
universe, more broadly.

There may also be spiritual practices within our religious or spiritual
traditions that we have never tried. I relish the opportunities to teach my
Christian college students about the beauty of lesser-known practices such
as meditating to music from the monastic community of Taizé, discerning
God's word using the practice of Lectio Divina, or walking a labyrinth (look
these up to learn more!). We enrich our engagement with our religious
traditions in ways that are nourishing and help us connect more deeply
when taking a pilgrimage, fasting, or celebrating different feasts or holy
days. Confession, communion, singing, praying with prayer beads, and
candle lighting can also be comforting and can help us feel more centered
spiritually. These intentional activities can be done alone or in community
with others. We can discover unique or under-utilized practices by speaking with our spiritual leaders or through researching our religious history.

There are also practices that might not be historically part of our own
religious or spiritual traditions that may help us grow closer to the Holy.
Some critics unkindly use the term "cafeteria religion" or "salad bar religion" to describe people's growing tendency to pick and choose whatever
religious beliefs and practices are interesting or amusing to them, but it is
possible that specific spiritual practices outside of our religious paradigms
may help us grow in faith and become more resilient. For some, straying
too far from explicitly condoned and sanctioned practices of our individual traditions can feel inauthentic and even sinful, so it is important that
we each discern for ourselves what is comfortable for us with regard to

15. Breslin and Lewis, "Theoretical Models," § "Abstract."

engaging in practices outside of our traditions. It is also essential that we treat those practices with reverence and respect, appreciating their value to the communities from which they originate. Examples might include candle lighting rituals, fasting, saying a prayer at mealtime, the practice of guided imagery, praying the Rosary, or a gratitude ritual. I personally feel that practices that help us grow closer to the Holy or feel more spiritually centered are not sinful and will support us during times of trial.

Whether we identify as religious or not, meditation is an example of a spiritual practice that can enhance our spiritual centeredness, improve our sense of connection to others and the universe, and provide comfort and calm. While meditation is a key element of the Noble Eightfold Path in Buddhism, it is not an exclusively religious practice.[16] It has been proven to lower blood pressure,[17] extend life expectancy,[18] and help people cope with suffering. It reduces feelings of anxiety, depression, and pain, and it increases feelings of empathy and creativity.[19] These benefits were illustrated in the powerful story of the twelve young soccer players and their coach Ekapol Chanthawong who were trapped in a flooded cave for over two weeks in Thailand. This young coach spent nearly half his life in a Buddhist monastery after being orphaned as a boy and learned the practice of meditation. When he and his team recognized their dire predicament, he began teaching them this important spiritual practice. This was credited for helping keep the players calm and alive during that difficult time.[20] It surely would have been less helpful had he been sitting in the cave thinking, "Well, now might be a good time for me to learn how to meditate!" Having this spiritual practice as an existing part of his "tool kit" was a lifesaving benefit for him and his team. Mindfulness meditation is based on the concept of being intentionally aware of our surroundings, our body, and our mind, and it invites us to be aware of the present moment, without the feelings of regret of what happened previously or the worry of what will happen next. There are meditation apps, programs, and retreats that can help us learn this important practice and help us become more resilient.

Spiritual or religious practices of all kinds can enable us to feel more centered and prepared for the storms of life, even practices that are not

16. Goldstein et al., "Current Perspectives," § 2, para 6.

17. Ibid., § 2.2, para 4.

18. Robert Schneider, cited in Adam, "Meditation," para. 5.

19. Brodwin, "Thai Cave Football Coach," paras. 7, 12, and 15.

20. Ibid., para. 2.

"spiritual practices" in a traditional sense. I once devised a unique ritual for a family member of one of my hospice patients. After the woman's death, her son felt the home had an air of unsettledness. We discussed his concerns, and I offered to conduct a short ritual that honored her life, blessed the home, and released her spirit, which brought comfort to the surviving son and helped him achieve a more peaceful sense of closure.

Isabella Baumfree, later known as Sojourner Truth, also used unique spiritual practices to cope with difficult circumstances; she was inspired and motivated by the practices of preaching and activism. She was born into slavery in upstate New York and was separated from her family when she was sold at age nine. After years of suffering and slavery, she and her baby daughter escaped. She had physical limitations, a painful history of abuse, innumerable setbacks and hardships, and spoke English as a second language, but she became a well-known public speaker and advocate, speaking about the evils of slavery, the importance of women's rights and non-violence, and the rights of freed slaves to own land, even meeting personally with President Lincoln.[21] She discovered that these spiritual practices of preaching and activism helped her not only cope with her circumstances, but also create incredible positive change for herself and the nation.

Spiritual practices can serve as buoys in times of distress, helping us stay afloat. Whether we recommit to familiar practices within our traditions that we have abandoned, try new ones that are associated with our traditions that we have yet to discover, or explore practices that are outside of our traditions, we will benefit from establishing some healthy habits that will help us feel spiritually centered or help us to grow closer to the Holy. An additional benefit of engaging in spiritual practices may be the development and refinement of our spiritual or religious beliefs, which can also serve as a source of comfort in times of difficulty.

SPIRITUAL OR RELIGIOUS BELIEFS

Just as our resilience can be bolstered from religious or spiritual community and practices, spiritual or religious beliefs can also provide comfort and inspiration. Holy writings and stories from different religious and spiritual traditions give witness to the strength and wisdom of role models

21. Truth, *Narrative*; *Biography.com*, s.v. "Sojourner Truth," https://www.biography.com/people/sojourner-truth-9511284.

and often testify to the benevolence and support of the Divine. Individuals from Judeo-Christian traditions sometimes hear this comforting verse at funerals: "Even though I walk through the darkest valley, I fear no evil; for you are with me; your rod and your staff—they comfort me."[22] The Islamic tradition also celebrates the presence and support of the Divine. One of the names for God in Islam is As-Samad, which can be translated as "Eternal Refuge" or "Satisfier of All Needs," and the Qur'an states, "They encountered suffering and adversity, and were so shaken in spirit that even the Messenger and those of faith who were with him cried: 'When (will come) the help of Allah?' Ah! Verily, the help of Allah is (always) near!"[23] The Qur'an also makes this assuring and comforting statement: "Verily, with every difficulty there is relief."[24] The Christian New Testament also offers assurances of support and encouragement. Jesus said this:

> Come to me, all you that are weary and are carrying heavy burdens, and I will give you rest. Take my yoke upon you, and learn from me; for I am gentle and humble in heart, and you will find rest for your souls. For my yoke is easy, and my burden is light.[25]

We are loved, and we are not alone on the journey through trials and traumas. We can discover comfort, peace, and resources from the Divine, from deep within ourselves, or from the universe.

Traditional holy writings are not the only place we can find inspiration. There are secular and spiritual quotations, stories, and readings that can serve as encouraging reminders and as tools for centering and discovering calm. Poetry, for instance, has the ability to speak to the depths of our hearts, and gifted poets such as Rumi, Mary Oliver, and Pablo Neruda have put to words some of our deepest griefs, hopes, worries, and observations. When I was struggling with life as a young adult, the "Footprints" poem was a deep comfort. It tells the story of a person who walks with God through life and sees both sets of footprints when looking back. The person notices only one set of footprints during the most trying times, and asks why. God assures the person that God was not absent during those trying times but was instead carrying the person. Even though it was a simple and fictional depiction, it was reassuring to me. Even social media has the capacity to

---

22. Ps 23:4 (NRSV).
23. Qur'an 2:214 (Yusuf Ali).
24. Qur'an 94:6 (Yusuf Ali).
25. Matt 11:28–30 (NRSV).

inspire from time to time, with endearing memes about positivity and hope that sometimes say what I need to hear in that moment. We can be inspired through many sources, if we are open to it.

Many resilient people throughout history were motivated to persevere by their spiritual or religious beliefs. Corazon Aquino, the president of the Philippines in the late 1980s and devoted Roman Catholic woman, faced adversity and hardship as she became the first female president of the Philippines through a non-violent revolution. Her inspiration to run for office stemmed from the assassination of her husband who spoke out against the ills of the country's long-term repressive president. With courage and determination, she helped democracy grow in that country, enabling the development of the country's constitution and the celebration of civil rights. She felt deeply motivated by her faith and "her very real sense that she [was] an instrument of God's will."[26] Even after her term, she fought against corruption and advocated for democratic principles alongside Catholic ally Cardinal Jaime Sin until her death.[27] Aquino said, "Faith is not simply a patience that passively suffers until the storm is past. Rather, it is a spirit that bears things—with resignations, yes, but above all, with blazing, serene hope."[28] Our beliefs can motivate and inspire us to endure even the most challenging circumstances.

Ultimately, our religious or spiritual beliefs inspire our faith, just as our faith is inspired by our religious or spiritual beliefs. Adversity tests our faith, but role models for faithfulness and spiritual fortitude can be found throughout many spiritual and religious traditions. An example from the Christian tradition is the ministry and lives of slaves in the American south. The slaves would gather for "bush meetings" where they would hear God's Word preached by a fellow slave, and they would sing religious spirituals while working endless hours on the plantations. They must have felt forgotten or neglected by God, but their faith was strong and helped them persevere through such terrible conditions. Imagine singing these words after having been physically or sexually abused, after being separated from your children, after hours and years of grueling, uncompensated work in the field:

> Sometimes I feel discouraged, and think my work's in vain,
> But then the Holy Spirit, revives my soul again.

26. Iyer, "Woman of the Year," 9.

27. "Obituary: Cardinal Jaime Sin," § "Man of Humor," para. 5.

28. Aquino, quoted in Iyer, "Woman of the Year," 9.

Don't ever feel discouraged, for Jesus is your friend,
And if you lack of knowledge, he'll ne'er refuse to lend.[29]

Even in the midst of hell on earth, when God was slow in answering prayer, not only were slaves maintaining their faith, but they were also evangelizing and worshiping, celebrating their faith and finding strength in it.

Their faith also inspired coordinated actions for justice. Although Harriet Tubman is perhaps the most well-known organizers, many people of faith played important roles in the courageous liberation work done by the Underground Railroad. Reverend Jehiel Berman, for instance, was the son of two former slaves who earned their freedom by fighting in the Revolutionary War. He was a pastor at a church in Connecticut in the mid-1800s that served as a stop on the Underground Railroad for slaves traveling to safety in Canada. The church earned the name "Freedom Church" because of the important role that it played, thanks to the courage of the pastor and parishioners.[30] The strength, courage, and wisdom derived from their spiritual beliefs and faith are inspiring.

Staying true to our belief systems and maintaining our faith is not always easy. Elie Wiesel, a Jewish author and advocate, survived unimaginable trauma while enduring imprisonment during the Holocaust as a teenager. In his unforgettable book *Night*, Wiesel uses these haunting and illuminating words to describe the depth of his suffering:

> Never shall I forget those flames which consumed my faith forever. Never shall I forget that nocturnal silence which deprived me, for all eternity, of the desire to live. Never shall I forget those moments which murdered my God and my soul and turned my dreams to dust. Never shall I forget these things, even if I am condemned to live as long as God Himself. Never.[31]

This quote sounds like a disavowal of God, but Wiesel did not give up on God; in fact, he wrestles with and confronts God about issues of suffering and injustice for the rest of his life. One scholar said, "It is to his credit that he is unwilling to retreat into easy atheism, just as he refuses to bury his head in the sand of optimistic faith. What Wiesel calls for is a fierce, defiant struggle with the Holocaust, and his work tackles a harder question: how

29. "There Is a Balm in Gilead."
30. *Freedom Church* (sign).
31. Wiesel, *Night*, 14.

is it possible not to believe in God after what happened?"[32] Muslim writer Yasmin Mogahed sees it this way:

> Your life is nothing more than a love story. Between you and God. Nothing more. Every person, every experience, every gift, every loss, every pain is sent to your path for one reason and one reason only: to bring you back to Him.[33]

Spiritual beliefs and faith can help us maintain our strength and discover hope even in the most challenging circumstances.

"DEEP CLEANSING BREATH"

My dear friend and academy classmate Jen says her faith is like a deep cleansing breath. God and religion were part of her life from a young age growing up in the Catholic Church. She found comfort in the familiar flow of the ceremony—kneeling, standing, singing, and reciting. She felt like a part of something bigger than just herself or her family or her neighborhood, saying, "Though I was a small part of a whole, I was a part of it in a meaningful way." She made the connection that organized religion could provide a sanctuary, literally and figuratively, of safety, consolation, and forgiveness.

She left the familiarity and comfort of her home and church when she graduated from high school and arrived at the Coast Guard Academy. Jen's small frame hides her physical strength and tenacity, and when she arrived at the academy, the sailing coach was quick to recruit her despite her inexperience. There she discovered a spiritual community of different sort in the tightly knit, competitive team. In sailing, she discovered rhythm, routine, and ritual. She felt connected to and dependent on her teammates. She felt the exultation of achievement and the intensity of disappointment throughout the season. There were occasions of seeking and giving forgiveness, and the team traveled together sharing their joys and sorrows. This new "congregation" of people fed her spirit during this time of spiritual homelessness.

Jen also discovered love on that team and connected with her teammate Greg who would eventually become her husband. His Protestant parents also raised him with a strong connection to the church, and she would

32. Henry, "Story and Silence," para. 3.

33. Mogahed, Facebook post, March 5, 2013.

periodically attend worship with his family at his home church not far from the academy.

Jen grew to admire and appreciate the male and female clergy she met, with their touching and thought-provoking sermons and abundant empathy. Once married, Greg and Jen decided to make this United Church of Christ congregation their home. On the day of their daughter's baptism years later, Jen's heart was overflowing with warmth, appreciation, and feelings of belonging and welcome as she watched the enthusiasm, love, and delight shown by Reverend Good and the congregation. When she was passing through a corridor soon after that baptism, she noticed for the first time a poem on the wall that speaks of faith and the miracles of nature, joy, and friendship that surround us. In this poem are these lines:

> How could I not [believe in God] when children laugh and even tears
> Bring meaning to the happiness that comes
> When trouble passes and the heart is still.[34]

As if the words were God's, she felt this poem call her more intentionally into this community of faith. She had found belonging in God and in this new spiritual home.

There would come a time, not long after, that this spiritual home would help cradle her deep woundedness. In the warm summer of 2011, Jen and Greg were a few weeks from giving birth to their second baby girl. At a routine appointment, the doctor was preforming the ultrasound and paused. In disbelief, the doctor declared that their baby girl had died in her womb, later to discover that there had been an unexpected umbilical cord accident. Jen delivered that beautiful baby in the silence of the early dawn of August 9, and she cradled Breila Stefanie Hall's precious body, admiring her beautiful dark hair, sweet button nose, and rosebud mouth. Jen wondered if she could ever feel joy again, laugh, or even smile. Their family, friends, and that beautiful community of faith helped her begin to heal, and as Jen said, "gathered the pieces of my world and gave them back to me." The church was a solid, consistent, and comforting place that served as a lifeline for Greg and Jen during that traumatic time, wrapping them in prayer and developing a beautiful and meaningful service to celebrate Breila's life. In addition to the support of the church community itself, Jen and Greg were bolstered by their belief in an eventual reunion with beautiful Breila, their

34. Johnston, "Credo," lines 18–20.

trust that God was present in their suffering, and the rituals and prayers that honored Breila's life that sustained Greg and Jen during this dark time.

Spiritual and religious communities, practices, and beliefs continue to sustain Jen as she sends her older daughter off to college and cares for animals in the veterinarian practice she has worked hard to build. Her spiritual groundedness and strength inspire others as she openly speaks about beautiful Breila and the grief they experienced, helping dispel the silence surrounding perinatal loss and stillbirth. Jen's spiritual and religious identity has helped her be more resilient and prepared for the unexpected changes and hardships of life.

FINAL THOUGHTS ON PIETY

Spiritual or religious communities, practice, and beliefs can help us become more resilient, and we benefit when we take time to explore, discover, and cultivate them in advance of a hardship or trauma. As we connect more deeply with spirituality or religion, we can begin to release feelings of fear and hopelessness and find peace. Hear these words of Buddhist monk Thich Nhat Hanh:

> Fear keeps us focused on the past or worried about the future. If we can acknowledge our fear, we can realize that right now we are okay. Right now, today, we are still alive, and our bodies are working marvelously. Our eyes can still see the beautiful sky. Our ears can still hear the voices of our loved ones.[35]

May we be inspired by our spiritual or religious communities, practices, and beliefs; may we release fear and despair; and may we live in the moment with confidence and peace.

REFLECTION AND ACTION

Questions to ponder

- How would you describe your connection to a spiritual or religious community, faith leader, and/or small group? Reflect on a time when you felt a sense of connection and support.

---

35. Nhat Hanh, *Fear*, 4.

- When have you had a sense of being loved and supported by a force greater than yourself?

- Which spiritual practices do you engage in consistently that are nourishing and meaningful? How do they make you feel?

- What has been your experience of yoga or meditation? If you have no experience, how might you introduce yourself to these practices?

- Which spiritually centered books or daily devotionals have been meaningful to you and why? If none, how might you find some recommendations for books you might enjoy?

- Which passages from your sacred writings are comforting to you? How do you characterize the Divine? The Muslim tradition uses ninety-nine names for God, including The Embodiment of Peace and The Ever-Acceptor of Repentance; what names would you use for the Divine?

Strategies for cultivating this characteristic of resilience

- Download a meditation app or find a meditation resource.

- Go online to learn more about the practice of walking a labyrinth. Find a labyrinth in your area and meditatively walk it.

- Participate in a yoga class or attend a yoga or meditation retreat.

- Connect with a spiritual or religious community. If you already have one, make an appointment to meet with your religious leader for coffee and find ways to connect more deeply with the community.

- Practice Lectio Divina or Imago Divina alone or with a friend. Research it online to learn more!

- Go on a religious or spiritual retreat or pilgrimage.

- Read poetry. Write poetry.

- Acquire a set of prayer beads and learn about different prayers that can be used with them or create your own prayer ritual using the beads.

- Reach out to a spiritual or religious leader to discuss lesser-known spiritual or religious practices that might help meet your spiritual needs and strengthen your spirit.

- Consider what justice issues you feel most passionate about and find ways to connect with communities in your area that are working on those issues.

- Create an intentional space at home that you can use for prayer, reading of holy writings, or meditation, perhaps with items that can help you focus and feel spiritually centered.

Prayer

Faithful Source of Life, we see signs of your companionship, love, and faithfulness. Help us to find our places in spiritual or religious communities that are loving, empowering, and supportive. Allow us to discover our ability to contribute to these communities as well as the willingness to receive blessings from them. Expose us to spiritual or religious practices that can help us grow closer to you, deepen our faith, and deepen our understanding of the role models who have gone before us. Inspire us to be faithful with these important spiritual practices. When we are despondent, help us to turn to our spiritual or religious stories and beliefs that can inspire, guide, and sustain us. Put on our hearts a strong faith in your love and in human goodness that can endure even during the darkest hours, and enable us to feel your presence, giving us warmth, and confidence. When our faith feels week and feeble, undergird it with your strength and compassion. As our faith grows and develops, may it be centered on your abundant love for us and your call to love our neighbors. Amen.

7

Perseverance

We must keep moving.
If you can't fly, run;
if you can't run, walk;
if you can't walk, crawl;
but by all means keep moving.

—MARTIN LUTHER KING JR.[1]

WE ARE ONLY ABLE to be transformed by hardship if we can survive it. *Perseverance* is the "continued effort to do or achieve something despite difficulties, failure, or opposition."[2] Maybe eating a whole "Granddaddy Moe" breakfast at my favorite diner takes some effort, but I wouldn't go so far as to say that it requires perseverance. Perseverance means not giving up on something, and it requires our commitment, dedication, and effort in unfavorable circumstances. Although some people seem inclined to think that the words *resilience* and *perseverance* are interchangeable, perseverance is one of the characteristics of resilience and is a pivotal element in many stories of resilience. While debating the relationship between *perseverance* and *resilience*, it is also worth distinguishing between *perseverance* and *grit*.

1. King, "Keep Moving."
2. *Merriam-Webster Online*, s.v. "Perseverance," https://www.merriam-webster.com/dictionary/perseverance.

Angela Duckworth describes grit as "sticking with things over the very long term until you master them," and says, "the gritty individual approaches achievement as a marathon; his or her advantage is stamina."[3] Grit is the quality of "stick-to-itiveness" or tenacity that enables us to persevere. Ultimately, in order to bounce back from trauma or difficulty, we have to simply get through it, no matter how long or difficult the journey may be. I sum it up this way: resilience requires perseverance; perseverance requires grit.

Like all the characteristics of resilience, the concept of perseverance is a theme in many religious and spiritual traditions. Many religions recognize the unavoidability of suffering and celebrate the spirit of perseverance that is required to endure and thrive. One of the Buddhist Noble Truths acknowledges the suffering in this world and inspires people to work toward the end of suffering.[4] Many of us discover this strength from the universe, from deep within ourselves, and from those around us. For those in theistic traditions—those belief systems centered around a higher power—we believe that our strength also comes from the Divine. The Muslim tradition, for instance, has a belief that God is closer to us than our jugular vein, and the Qur'an also says, "God is sufficient for us; an excellent Guardian is He."[5] Similarly, the Hebrew Bible says, "May the Lord give strength to his people! May the Lord bless his people with peace!"[6] We have sources of strength that can and will help us remain hopeful and persevere. We can be comforted with the assurance that we are not forsaken, forgotten, or discarded.

Laura Hillenbrand's powerful biography *Unbroken* helps us learn more about an incredible story of perseverance.[7] Louis Zamperini was a talented young man who discovered a love for running and competed in the five-kilometer race in the 1936 Olympics, demonstrating an incredibly high level of physical strength and durability. Several years later, he entered the Army Air Corps and served during World War II as a bombardier on a B-24. During that time, his bomber crashed at sea. He survived over a month on a life raft, wondering if he would be rescued and by whom. In an unbelievable turn for the worse, he was "rescued" by the enemy and then endured two years of extreme torture and deprivation in a prison camp.

---

3. Hanford, "Angela Duckworth," para. 2.
4. "Basics of Buddhism," § "The Four Noble Truths."
5. Qur'an 3:173 (Arberry).
6. Ps 29:11 (NRSV).
7. Hillenbrand, *Unbroken*.

Day to day, he figured out how to survive and endure in spite of the suffering. Even after his release, his son reported that memories of his captivity and torture continued to haunt him, and he used alcohol to try to cope. His deep suffering negatively affected his relationships and life, but a sermon by Reverend Billy Graham profoundly impacted him, renewed his faith, and helped transform his life.[8] Through difficult times, while sometimes coping imperfectly, Louie Zamperini was a model of strength and perseverance. In his life story, he demonstrated the two important elements of perseverance: mental endurance and physical endurance.

MENTAL ENDURANCE

There is an enormous mental component to perseverance. Many Ironman triathletes and ultramarathoners agree that their mindset is a critical piece of succeeding when their body is being challenged to its limits. Mental endurance is a frame of mind that is oriented to persistence, tenacity, and survival. It involves a determination and steadfastness that focuses on the belief that we *can* and *will* complete the task, despite the suffering. Mental endurance also takes into account the likelihood that the suffering will not last forever. This mental toughness can be cultivated by doing these five practices: committing to a goal, embracing a growth mindset, pursuing education, believing in ourselves, and exercising patience.

Committing to a goal is a powerful way to discover increased mental durability. This goal could be running a marathon or earning a college degree. For some of us, though, our goals may seem less lofty but might be vital for our very existence—surviving a depressive episode, enduring the loss of a partner or child, or withstanding a natural disaster. When a goal seems overwhelming, one strategy is to set shorter-term goals that service the overall goal. While a cadet at the Coast Guard Academy, my obvious goal was to graduate, but I honestly detested the first year of indoctrination, hazing, and subordination. I deliberated daily: "Should I leave or stay?" Realizing that this was time consuming, energy draining, and unproductive, my parents encouraged me to establish specific short-term goals. Instead of looking to graduation four years in the future, I identified chronological milestones at which times I would allow myself to consider leaving. After making it to my first milestone of Thanksgiving break, I considered my options, discussed it with my family, and resolved to stay at least until

8. Ong, "Louis Zamperini's Son," paras. 8, 11–13.

Christmas. I spent the next few weeks focused on studying, building relationships, developing coping strategies, and discovering life-giving activities like playing on the volleyball team and hanging out with my women friends at our favorite dive, Captain's Pizza. At Christmas, the decision to stay came a bit easier, and so on. Next thing I knew, I was walking across the stage with a fraction of the cadets who reported in with me four years earlier, shaking hands with commencement speaker President Bill Clinton. Making short-term goals was critical for me.

A far more rigorous program is Navy SEAL training. The physical and intellectual standards for qualifying for the Navy SEALs are extraordinary, and only a small number of applicants are even eligible for the year-long training. The most demanding part of the training is one specific period called Hell Week, where trainees are engaged in grueling physical activity for nearly twenty hours per day, experience substantial physical and emotional pain, and get only a few hours of sleep. If they decide to resign from the program or "Drop on Request," they ring a brass bell three times. Only about one in four candidates makes it to the end of Hell Week.[9]

One thing that differentiates those who stay and those who leave is believed to be their goal setting. The candidates who are most likely to quit resign in the first few days because they are looking at the length of the program and are saying to themselves, "I can't possibly keep this up until the end." Alternately, the more successful candidates tend to focus on short-term goals like making it to the next meal or even just surviving the next few minutes.[10]

Short-term goals are realistic and attainable, and achieving them can inspire us to continue on the journey. A woman I met recently said she used a similar strategy to cope with the death of her daughter who died by suicide. She knew she needed to put all of her energy into "putting one foot in front of the other," as she said, day by day to prevent herself from being overwhelmed by grief. Alcoholics Anonymous also recognizes the importance of short-term goal setting and has adopted the saying "One day at a time" to help prevent people from feeling overwhelmed by the daunting task of a long lifetime of sobriety. Just focusing on today is enough. We can focus on tomorrow then. Short-term goals will help us move toward our larger goal.

9. Harris et al., "BUDS," 2.

10. Marshall, "Lessons from the SEALs," § "How SEALs Survive."

Our mental endurance also benefits from embracing a growth mindset. A growth mindset is a frame of mind that enables us to see our mistakes and failures as opportunities for learning and growth, believing that ability and intellect are not fixed things, but instead are qualities that can be developed through effort and hard work.[11] Michael Jordan, one of the most talented basketball players in history said this: "I've missed more than 9,000 shots in my career. I've lost almost 300 games. 26 times, I've been trusted to take the game winning shot and missed. I've failed over and over and over again in my life. And that is why I succeed."[12] Successful and accomplished people admit to—and even laugh about—their failures, recognizing that failure helps fuel their motivation to work harder and enables them to recognize ways in which they can improve and grow.

At my kids' swim team banquet last year, their coach Rob talked about how much he enjoyed establishing and coaching the team of hard-working athletes alongside his dedicated and talented spouse. He also shared that when he was a young coach looking for a coaching job in college athletics, he would keep all the rejection letters that he received from athletics departments to motivate himself, using the rejections to encourage his learning and find inspiration.[13] He teaches his athletes that hard work and dedication are the keys to athletic and personal success and fulfillment, and he serves as a role model for that in his life as a police officer and in his coaching. He says this to his athletes: "If the side of a mountain were smooth, no one would ever get to the top. Use the obstacles in your way to push yourself forward."[14] A growth mindset supports mental endurance because it allows us to recognize our ability to positively influence our own outcomes through the power of hard work and practice. This empowers us to persevere.

A third, and maybe surprising, element of mental endurance is education. Scientists studied resilience in people who survived the tsunami in Indonesia in 2004. Five years after the storm, survivors with higher levels of education were in "better psycho-social health" than their less educated peers and concluded that "education is associated with higher levels of

11. *Glossary of Education Reform*, s.v. "Growth Mindset," https://www.edglossary.org/growth-mindset/.

12. Goldman and Papson, *Nike Culture*, 49.

13. Riccobon, speech.

14. Riccobon, email message to author, November 6, 2018.

resilience over the longer term."[15] Education also affects situations that are more commonplace. One study showed that college-educated women are nearly twice as likely as those with a high school education to still be married to their partner after twenty years[16] and, at the same time, are more likely to escape marriages that are abusive or violent.[17] Among those who do divorce, educated women, even those not working outside the home, discover higher levels of economic security after the divorce.[18] Pursuing education is worthwhile and will increase our resilience. Even though it can prove difficult for those of us who are struggling financially or lack self-confidence, making our education a priority is something we can do to prepare for life's setbacks.

We also improve our mental endurance by believing in ourselves, even when others might doubt us. A good example of this is Theodor Seuss Geisel, better known as Dr. Seuss. Dr. Seuss's books are a staple in many American households. His rhymes and rhythm, the relevance and depth of the content, and his incredible sense of humor are unmatched. Surprisingly, Dr. Seuss encountered many doubters on his journey from advertising employee to world-famous author. His first book, *And to Think That I Saw It on Mulberry Street*, was rejected by over two dozen publishers, but he believed in the value of his work and continued to seek a publisher when other authors might have quit. One life-changing day, he had just left yet another publisher's office after suffering the most recent rejection when he bumped into a college friend who happened to be a new employee at a publishing company nearby. When the friend invited Geisel to his office for one last look, Geisel agreed, and they signed a publishing contract that day.[19] Dr. Seuss went on to sell over six hundred million books.[20] His belief in himself helped him persevere, making it possible for his compassion and wisdom to be a blessing to many.

Whether we are trying to be a successful author, loving parent, high-achieving athlete, or just hoping to pass a course or survive the day without crying, believing in ourselves is critical. We are rarely going to receive the

15. Frankenberg et al., "Education, Vulnerability," 16.

16. Wang, "Link," para. 2.

17. Kreager et al., "Women's Education," para. 6.

18. Peterson, *Women, Work, and Divorce*, 90.

19. "Biography"; Grazer and Fishman, *Curious Mind*, excerpted in "The Book No One Would Publish."

20. Winerip, "Mulberry Street," para. 6.

affirmation we need (or deserve!) from others, but if we believe in ourselves and refuse to give up, we will learn, grow, and succeed. Lily Herman, a recent graduate of Wesleyan University, put it well in an article she wrote for the university's magazine about the *thousand* articles she wrote during her time there. In this article, she describes the first seven hundred articles as bad or mediocre, but she persevered and produced three hundred more of which she was proud, or in her humble words, "things started to look good." Lily said, "If I could give one piece of advice to anyone, it's that you can overcome a lot in this industry . . . when you let go of the feeling that your self-worth is tied to any one 'thing' you create."[21] Believing in ourselves, even when we make mistakes or fail, gives us the fortitude and incentive to press forward and to try again—to have the mental endurance to persevere.

Mental endurance also requires patience. Patience is becoming increasingly rare in our on-demand culture. When we wait on line, we can distract ourselves with our long list of unread messages. When we are flying across country, we can binge-watch our favorite TV shows. When we eat lunch, we catch up on the world news or the images on social media. I feel anxious and impatient when I arrive somewhere early. Even a few minutes of time feels like such a waste, and I wonder about what other chores and tasks I could have checked off my list instead of arriving early, which is why I'm always barely on time (or late!). We are not accustomed to waiting, and we have lost the art of being patient. This lack of patience and our decreasing attention spans have gained the interest of researchers who have determined that our attention span is now even shorter than that of a goldfish.[22] Many are working to fight these trends with the "slow" movement. Slow Food and even Slow Cocktails and Slow Beer movements are gaining popularity, and some are promoting the Slow Reading Movement, where we can nurture our minds through indulging in long-form, old-fashioned literature, which takes time and investment but also cultivates our sense of empathy, our happiness, and our intelligence.[23]

Patience is a critical piece of resilience. Sadly, when we are facing unwanted change, hardship, or grief, we are often put in a place of waiting. We are waiting for the test results to see if treatment is working, waiting for the suffocating grief to subside, waiting for the job offer we've been seeking, or maybe waiting for a call from an adult child. Perhaps because of his own

21. Herman, "How I Wrote," 11.

22. Statistic Brain, quoted in David, "Why Waiting Is Hard," para. 3.

23. Kelly, "Slow-Books Manifesto," paras. 1, 3–4.

experience waiting, Dr. Seuss captures this beautifully in his book *Oh, the Places You'll Go* when he writes about "the Waiting Place" and highlights the many times and places we will find ourselves waiting, from waiting for the bus to waiting for a "Better Break."[24] Waiting is impossibly hard, but there are secular, spiritual, and religious sources of inspiration around us.

Holy writings from the Jewish and Christian traditions refer to the importance of patience. In the book of Genesis, we hear a story about Jacob working patiently for a total of fourteen years to earn the privilege of marrying Rachel, the woman he truly loved. The book of Proverbs reminds us that "patience brings peace,"[25] and the book of Lamentations says, "The Lord is good to everyone who trusts in him, so it is best for us to wait in patience . . . When we suffer, we should sit alone in silent patience."[26] In the Christian New Testament, the apostle Paul talked about patience in his letters, calling it the "fruit of the Spirit"[27] and inviting the readers to "lead a life worthy of the calling to which you have been called, with all humility and gentleness, with patience, bearing with one another in love."[28] He also encouraged the fledgling Roman church to "be patient in suffering."[29] Hinduism, Taoism, and Buddhism all celebrate patience and see it as a virtue.[30] Islam also places deep value on patience and believes that the ability to be patient comes from God. People in the Muslim community are invited to "persevere in patience and constancy,"[31] and elsewhere in the Qur'an, one translation beautifully says, "So be patient with gracious patience."[32]

Demonstrating gracious patience is a beautiful ambition. Sometimes I feel like a religious failure because of my inability to be patient at all, let alone demonstrate "gracious patience." The Christian Bible invites me to trust in God completely, and being patient with God and my circumstances should be a natural byproduct of that trust. While my spirit takes comfort in those assuring verses and encouragements, my Type-A self is terrified about the prospect of waiting, particularly in a place of discomfort, pain, or

24. Geisel, *Oh, the Places*, 23–25.

25. Prov 15:18 (GNT).

26. Lam 3:25–28 (GNT).

27. Gal 5:22 (NRSV).

28. Eph 4:1–2 (NRSV).

29. Rom 12:12 (NRSV).

30. Schnitker and Emmons, "Patience," 180.

31. Qur'an 3:200 (Yusuf Ali).

32. Qur'an 70:5 (Sahih International).

unknowing. I don't think I'm alone in this! In one study, there was a definite correlation between a belief in the "importance of patience" and religiousness, but *no* correlation between religiousness and actually being patient![33]

Perhaps our aversion to being patient is precisely because patience is often associated with discomfort or suffering. The Greek word commonly translated as "patience" that is used in parts of the New Testament is *makrothymia* and is sometimes translated as "longsuffering."[34] That translation acknowledges the difficulty or sadness sometimes experienced during our times of waiting, but we are not powerless during our waiting. Researchers said this: "Patience should not be conceptualized as passive resignation or learned helplessness, but instead as an assertive acceptance of waiting."[35] While the misery is sometimes very real, it is helpful to our resilience if we regulate our emotions and reactions and use our waiting time to proactively focus on our sources of hope. Our hope comes from the expectation that when the waiting is over, our suffering will diminish, a solution will be discovered, or our goal will be reached. Catholic priest and philosopher Thomas Aquinas said, "A person is said to be patient . . . because he acts in a praiseworthy manner by enduring things which hurt him here and now and is not unduly saddened by them."[36] Patience, along with focusing on our goals, embracing a growth mindset, pursuing education, and believing in ourselves, will help increase our mental endurance and enable us to feel and be more resilient. Our mental endurance is not the only aspect of perseverance that needs cultivating; physical endurance is just as essential.

PHYSICAL ENDURANCE

The physical endurance seen in the stories of climbers of Mt. Everest are truly unbelievable. In his book *Into Thin Air*, Jon Krakauer details the suffering, persistence, and tenacity of the climbers as they strive to achieve their goal of summiting the highest mountain in the world while facing the prospect of mortal injury, frostbite, interpersonal strife, and crushing fear. [37] They demonstrated extraordinary endurance, and in working toward their goal, they discovered who they were, learned about their own

33. Schnitker and Emmons, "Patience," 190.
34. *Strong's Concordance*, s.v. "Makrothumia," https://biblehub.com/greek/3115.htm.
35. Schnitker and Emmons, "Patience," 201.
36. Aquinas, quoted in ibid., 177.
37. Krakauer, *Into Thin Air*.

abilities and strengths, and presumably felt more able to face future difficulties. Physical endurance is a key to resilience that we can cultivate through physical fitness, sleep, and self-care.

Our physical fitness is a key to resilience, and we have the power to improve it. Exercise releases endorphins that help our mental health, builds our strength and cardiovascular endurance, and extends our life expectancy. Unfortunately, fitness is often set aside when we are feeling overwhelmed and overworked. According to recent data, two-thirds of adults are considered overweight or obese, and one in six children suffer from obesity.[38] When we think of terrifying scenarios like those portrayed in the television show *The Walking Dead*, the people who seem most likely to survive are those who are fit and healthy. This is backed up by data. When Hurricane Maria hit Puerto Rico in the fall of 2017, there were about sixty-four people who died during the storm, but a year after the disaster, the death toll rose to nearly three thousand. This profound loss of life included the deaths of those who were cut off from medical care and those who had chronic medical conditions that they were unable to treat properly given the lack of power and access to medical facilities and healthcare professionals. Healthier people who had fewer medical needs fared better, and their physical fitness and wellness enabled them to begin to bounce back more easily from the traumatic and life-changing event. While there are potential health conditions over which we have no control, we will have a greater ability to persevere if we strive to be as healthy and fit as possible.

Physical fitness not only enables us to physically withstand trauma better, it also has therapeutic benefits. Even as early as the early 1900s, scientists proved that exercise had a direct benefit on mental health, a conclusion that was reinforced in a recent study that showed that exercise decreases symptoms of depression, even among those struggling with clinical depression.[39] In fact, the elite soccer player Nadia Nadim was introduced to the sport of soccer because it served as a comforting, fun, and helpful escape from the stress of living in a refugee camp in Denmark after she and her family fled their native Afghanistan following her father's murder.[40] Similarly, teenage girls can be seen laughing and playing soccer together outside Mumbai where they discover their physical power and inner strength through this empowering sport after it was brought to the neighborhood by

38. "Overweight," § "Fast Facts."
39. Craft and Perna, "Benefits," § "Summary."
40. "Refugee Soccer Star."

a non-governmental agency.[41] Physical fitness has significant physical and mental benefits that help our ability to persevere.

Just as physical fitness benefits our wellness, good sleep habits are another critical element of increasing our physical endurance. Although this may seem simplistic, sleep is an essential component of happiness and health, and more than half of us are lacking this important "medicine." Although opinions vary, studies show that we generally need between seven and eight hours of sleep a night. Positive psychology books talk about its importance in happiness and coping, and evidence proves that adequate sleep reduces the effects of stress on our well-being and enables us to better regulate our emotions.[42] Too little sleep is blamed for weight problems, depression, heart disease, and even dying sooner.[43] Although sleep often feels luxurious and self-indulgent, it will help us live longer, be happier, and discover increased resilience.

Also criticized for being self-indulgent is self-care, another critical aspect of physical endurance. We often characterize self-care as a luxury of the privileged, and we see self-care as self-satisfying practices that help us feel good or escape our difficult realities. This is not true. Self-care is the act of doing what we need to sustain our bodies, minds, and spirits, *not* for the purpose of self-indulgence or superficial pleasure, but for the purpose of continuing the fight for survival and the pursuit of justice. Self-care practices are those that nourish us, educate us, inspire us, and renew us. When we eliminate self-care practices, we risk increased suffering and decreased resilience. We may convince ourselves that our priorities are in the *right* place by prioritizing others over ourselves or by focusing on our goals instead of our well-being, but actually, we disadvantage ourselves and others. Here is an analogy: I was recently jogging and felt exhausted. Although I was barely making forward progress, I was determined to keep jogging. When I couldn't run for even one more second, I decided to walk for a bit. After that short walk, I was *full* of energy. At the end of my jog, my pace was much faster overall because of my short break. Self-care doesn't detract from our productivity, but actually makes us *more* productive.

What constitutes self-care is personal and unique for each individual. A recent article touted the benefits of crafts and handiwork, more technically referred to as "purposeful hand use." These seemingly old-fashioned

41. "Football."

42. Weinberg et al., "Sleep Well," 91.

43. Williams, "How Much," para. 3.

practices such as knitting, gardening, woodworking, and sewing are proven to help us manage stress, depression, and anxiety. The author argued the following:

> Too much time on technological devices and the fact that we buy almost all of what we need rather than having to make it has deprived us of processes that provide pleasure, meaning and pride. Making things promotes psychological well-being. Process is important for happiness because when we make, repair or create things we feel vital and effective.[44]

For others, jogging, yoga, or other forms of exercise or movement are types of self-care that help enhance physical endurance. Research shows that even laughing can be a form of self-care because it is related to the releasing of endorphins, better blood flow, reduced pain and blood sugar levels, improved sleep, and a stronger immune system.[45] Whether it is journaling, drawing, walking, playing with pets, meditating, baking, or attending a comedy show, we benefit from discovering and practicing those activities that help us feel renewed and enlivened. Ultimately, whether we like it or not, true self-care rarely (if ever!) involves technology or social media, and our use of technology could be working against our wellness. Cutting our online time and using that time for nourishing self-care practices would likely help us become more resilient. One of the most important ways to exercise self-care, however, is to recognize when it is time to change direction.

PERSEVERANCE VERSUS QUITTING

Sometimes perseverance can be confused with stubbornness or inflexibility. Defining perseverance as "not quitting" is far too simplistic. Sometimes, when we're going down the wrong road, turning around is exactly what we must do. Turning around or changing course is *not* quitting. It does *not* reflect a lack of perseverance but instead is a decision that is made based on the information available that is telling us that a new strategy is needed or that the effort we're putting into something is not worth the benefit. When I was considering resigning from the Coast Guard, I didn't want to be a quitter. I told myself that the most powerful way to change the hostile aspects of military culture was from within. I worried that resigning would

44. Barron, "Creativity," para. 1.
45. MacDonald, "Laughter," § "Medical Benefits."

be detrimental to my female colleagues and mentors and would disappoint the many people who supported me. But staying in would have required me to end a meaningful personal relationship, and, worse, staying in meant living with demoralizing sexual harassment and emotional abuse. I knew in my spirit that staying in would cause irreparable harm to my mental health and overall well-being. I determined that resigning was my best option. Did I quit? Well, yes, in the eyes of some, but I have worked hard over many years to see my departure from military service as a mature, rational, wise choice to put my ego aside and to take a healthier and more life-affirming path. I have been deeply comforted by words from a potent and insightful folk song named "Seize the Day" that was written and sung by dear friends:

> Get past the let down, let down the heavy load. Know when to turn around no matter how long you've been on the wrong road. Got to know when to dig in, dig in and make your stand. Got to know when giving in gives you the upper hand.[46]

We often feel so invested in a choice that reversing course seems so difficult, but the imagery in this insightful song is powerful: if we are on a road that isn't right for us, no amount of walking is going to put us in the place we need to be. Changing course is sometimes an essential part of perseverance.

"MY FATHER WOULD HAVE WANTED ME TO FINISH WHAT I STARTED"

Andrea is feisty, funny, strident, and loving. The determined bounce in her step is matched by her effervescent brunette curls and warm smile. We were kindred spirits from the moment we met at the Coast Guard Academy, and I depended heavily on her strength and fortitude as we celebrated the good times and consoled each other during the challenging ones. In every way, Andrea has been an example of perseverance—showing her mental and physical endurance in the many twists and turns she endured.

Her strength and determination were tested mid-way through her four years at the academy when she and four friends were falsely accused of engaging in sexual conduct in a government vehicle. It was an exceptionally low point for Andrea, who had worked so hard to excel and was tormented by the judgment, marginalization, and shaming that resulted from this event. She didn't know who to trust and found herself being more

46. Thompson and Thompson, "Seize the Day."

severely punished than the others, worsening her feeling of injustice and persecution. She decided, though, that she had enough of the feelings of despondency and frustration, and she began to do what was necessary for her to emerge from that dark time. She focused on academics and prioritized the activities that brought her joy and fulfillment. With mindfulness and determination, she felt stronger than ever a semester later. That strength she discovered would be needed throughout her life, and it helped solidify her tenacious spirit.

Andrea is a fighter, which has been an asset given her choice of vocation. After completing her two years of sea duty following our academy graduation, Andrea became a rescue helicopter pilot. She served in the Coast Guard for over twenty years, where she persevered through fear, fog, and the still-strong old boys' network. Andrea demonstrated incredible perseverance professionally as she worked alongside mostly male colleagues, traveled to Antarctica, endured long deployments, and flew missions throughout many nights. She tolerated repetitive moves across country, tearing herself away from support systems and friends, and she endured the painful and life-changing experience of divorce, requiring her to rediscover her identity and financial independence.

One of Andrea's sources of strength and inspiration was her father, who was also a pilot. In addition to his love of flying, she inherited his laugh, sense of humor, and strong work ethic. They were incredibly close, understood each other, and shared a deep mutual appreciation. Nothing could have prepared her for the call she received while she and her aircraft were deployed on a Coast Guard ship in a remote part of the Arctic. Her dad was in a serious bicycle accident while on a business trip in Switzerland, and he was hospitalized and unresponsive. She immediately made arrangements to get to Geneva, needing to make six stops on the long and desperate journey to be at his bedside.

During this trip, she encountered a flight attendant who recognized her angst and grief. The woman gave her a special seat near the exit of the plane and ensured that Andrea didn't miss her connecting flight. In a memorable and poignant moment, the flight attendant held Andrea's hand and said a prayer in her Native American tradition for Andrea and her father. Andrea was deeply touched and strengthened for the rest of the journey. She joined her mother and sister in Geneva, where they made the impossibly difficult decision to remove her father from life support. As she traveled back to the United States after his death, her unit commander gave her the choice of either heading back to her home base in Alabama or returning to her deployment. Within weeks of her father's passing, Andrea was back on deployment, ready to fly and serve, honoring her dad's memory with her perseverance and dedication to duty and also knowing that it was what her father would have wanted her to do.

Throughout Andrea's life and career, she has had a laser focus on the mission, but she also had the insight to identify injustice and the courage to call it out. This characteristic proved to be both a gift and liability in her career, particularly when she found herself both the survivor of sexual harassment and the demonized plaintiff in a case against her hostile supervisor who had bullied her and treated her unfairly. The adjudication of the case was time-consuming and humiliating, leading to further loneliness and marginalization at an already-toxic assignment. She did not receive the justice she deserved, but Andrea found comfort in a local therapist who helped her process her feelings. She completed her assignment with honor and resolve, but her supervisor gave her a negative evaluation which she knew would eventually prevent her promotion and ultimately lead to a forced retirement. She thought things couldn't get worse, but when she arrived at her next unit, she discovered that the leadership of her former unit recommended she be grounded and undergo a psychiatric evaluation because of the emotional help she sought and received. Still, Andrea persevered and worked hard to successfully show her new boss the extent of her skills, ability, commitment, and determination.

She used that experience to learn and grow—finding sources of support, discovering a healthier work-life balance, appropriately compartmentalizing when needed, and creating her own definition of success that takes into account effort and heart. She was reminded of the importance of celebrating who she is and honoring her values. She now flies emergency medical helicopters in the civilian sector, rescuing people in the most desperate and dangerous circumstances, still persevering through the literal and figurative storms of life. She beautifully summarized the importance of perseverance in the speech she gave at her Coast Guard retirement ceremony:

> Everyone who works in the Coast Guard for twenty years has their challenges, and I'm certainly no exception. But without those challenges, I would not have the clarity of perspective to know my strengths. Without the times when I felt so alone, I would not recognize who my true friends are. Without the times when

I was faced with hard decisions, I wouldn't know that when the time comes to make a choice between doing the right thing *or* the easy thing, I will have the moral courage to choose the right thing. Without those challenges, I wouldn't have learned one of the most valuable lessons in life—that it is not the falling down that counts, but the way in which you choose to get back up. I am also grateful for the challenges; they are part of the experience that has made me a better, more confident person and pilot, and I wouldn't have had it any other way.[47]

Andrea lives life to its fullest. She consistently and fearlessly demonstrates physical and mental endurance and truly embodies resilience.

FINAL THOUGHTS ON PERSEVERANCE

Our ability to persevere depends on developing our mental and physical endurance. Like ducks, we may appear to glide along blissfully and gracefully, but underwater, we are often kicking like mad, and we might be wondering how much further we can go. With resolve, intentionality, and practice, each of us can go much further than we think. We can discover our inner strength and continue to build our mental and physical endurance that will enable us to persevere and thrive.

REFLECTION AND ACTION

Questions to ponder

- What sorts of traumas and difficulties have you endured in the past? What internal and external resources did you access in order to persevere?

- Reflect on times that you gave up easily on tasks and also times that you were determined to find solutions. What sorts of things motivated your choices? What inspired you to quit or to persevere?

- Consider your level of physical fitness and your exercise regimen. If there is room for improvement, what might you do differently to become physically healthier and stronger?

---

47. Sacchetti, retirement speech.

- What practices do you engage in that enhance your overall wellness such as meditation, yoga, or regular prayer practices? What practices might you introduce into your life?

- Describe your relationship with your therapist, counselor, or spiritual director. What do they provide? If you do not have one, how might you go about connecting with these important, objective resources?

- Describe your internal and external resources and gifts.

Strategies for cultivating this characteristic of resilience

- Do something outside of your comfort zone such as registering for a race, doing a strenuous hike, or riding an amusement park ride.

- Do something spontaneous.

- Journal about how your failures have helped you grow and learn and how they have led to new opportunities or relationships.

- Find something you love or are curious about and take a class that is offered through a local high school, college, town, or library.

- Practice patience by waiting in a waiting room or on a checkout line without the distraction of a smart phone or even a magazine.

- Set a fitness goal such as a "couch to 5K" program, working with an athletic trainer, taking a fitness class, or walking regularly.

- Make an appointment for an annual physical exam.

- Keep track of your sleep schedule, aiming for eight to nine hours. Avoid caffeine and screen time before bed, and work to develop a relaxing bedtime ritual that invites relaxation and peacefulness.

- Schedule some things that may involve not meeting all your creature comforts but are rewarding such as a long hike, camping, or backpacking.

- Take a yoga class and practice holding poses that are slightly outside your comfort zone.

- Discover what helps you feel renewed and refreshed, and schedule time for those activities.

- Attend a meditation class or meditation retreat.

- Keep a journal where you can write down your long-term goals and then list the achievable short-term goals that will help you achieve those long-term goals. Check off the short-term goals as they are accomplished as a way of ritualizing your progress. You may also benefit from setting up rewards for yourself for along the way!

- If you are working toward a long-term goal, share that goal with someone you trust and have them check in with you regularly to help keep you accountable. Establish shorter-term goals on which you can focus as you work toward that long-term goal.

Prayer

Spirit of Resolve and Strength, from the beginning of time, you have not abandoned us. You have been on this journey with us, helping us through the darkest times, enabling us to discover strength we did not know was within us. Please, God of Might, continue to be with us in ways that we can experience and feel. Remind us of your love and dedication through the voices and kindness of others. Allow us to discover our inner strength, and motivate us to develop our mental and physical endurance to help us be better prepared for what awaits. When we feel disheartened, despondent, or exhausted, breathe new life into our bodies and spirits. Provide us the discipline we need to care for our minds, bodies, and spirits. Inspire us to make our wellness a priority so we have the strength to love and serve others. Help enliven our faith and our closeness to you. Amen.

Closing Thoughts

You will make all kinds of mistakes;
but as long as you are generous and true, and also fierce,
you cannot hurt the world or even seriously distress her.

—Winston Churchill[1]

RESILIENCE IS A SIMPLE set of characteristics that you can continuously cultivate to enable you to be emotionally, cognitively, and spiritually prepared for and transformed by trauma, disappointment, and difficulty. I hope that the information, practices, strategies, and exercises provided will help you feel better equipped for whatever you may face. I hope that you feel capable and inspired, because you are an incredible creation, and you *do* have the ability to become more peaceful and prepared for the stormy seas of life.

Where do you start? If it feels overwhelming, simply start somewhere! Start anywhere! Remember the quote of the Taoist philosopher Lao Tzu, "The journey of a thousand miles begins with a single step."[2] Decide which of these Ps gives you the most energy and makes you most excited. Then start with one habit you can add, eliminate, or change. Voila! You are on your way to increasing your resilience! Let's review the characteristics that constitute resilience and how we can work toward building each characteristic:

1. Churchill, *My Early Life*, 60.
2. Lao Tzu, quoted in Ming-Dao, *Each Journey*, Intro., para. 4.

- *People*: We can strive to build social connections and identify and develop authentic relationships with encouraging and empowering individuals, communities, mentors, mentees, and role models.

- *Positivity*: We can take seriously the benefits of positive thinking and better manage worry and fear by retraining our minds to focus on the positive when we look at ourselves and others and when we reflect on our past, present, and future circumstances.

- *Pliability*: We can successfully brave the unwanted and unexpected changes associated with hardship by acknowledging our new reality and by living into the new reality by reserving judgment, managing anxiety, and embracing hope.

- *Problem Solving*: We can discover solutions to large and small problems by identifying our overarching goals, clearly defining the problems that need solving, doing our research, making a plan, and assessing our outcomes.

- *Purpose*: We can become more focused, intentional, and durable by defining and developing our sense of purpose by exploring our identities, honoring our experiences, defining our beliefs, discerning what brings us joy, assessing our gifts and skills, and having an open mind.

- *Piety*: We can seek grounding and inspiration in faith, religion, or spirituality by connecting with communities, by engaging in meaningful and life-giving spiritual practices, and by discovering comforting and energizing spiritual or religious beliefs.

- *Perseverance*: We can find the strength and ability to endure—and even thrive—in challenging circumstances by improving upon our mental and physical endurance.

FURTHER CONSIDERATIONS

There are a few more aspects worth highlighting. First, cultivating our resilience does not require us to become people we are not. We are not being inauthentic when we work to be mindful of our thoughts, behaviors, and habits and adjust them in the effort to become wiser and more durable. We already have much of what we need inside of us to become more resilient. When we choose to make resilience-building a lifestyle, we are simply identifying and fine-tuning our existing gifts and skills, we are recognizing the areas that need a bit of extra attention, and we are employing strategies that help us grow more fully into our mature, integrated, capable selves.

Second, resilience has nothing to do with success or failure. Our culture places a large emphasis on achievement and accomplishment, but the truly resilient person survives and thrives regardless of the end result. Reverend Bonhoeffer was no less resilient because his life was ended early by his execution. Boxer Joe Louis was resilient, even though he died in poor emotional and physical health and without any money. One of the incredible women highlighted in one of the chapters did not successfully graduate from the Coast Guard Academy, and another was forced to retire. Our outcomes may not always fit the mold of "success" as it might be defined by us, by those close to us, or by our communities. That does not mean we aren't resilient; in fact, it just might mean that we are *more* resilient because we have more real-life opportunities to practice and test these important characteristics when things have gone abysmally wrong. President Theodore Roosevelt said this:

> The credit belongs to the man who is actually in the arena, whose face is marred by dust and sweat and blood; who strives valiantly; who errs, who comes short again and again, because there is no effort without error and shortcoming; but who does actually strive to do the deeds; who knows great enthusiasms, the great devotions; who spends himself in a worthy cause; who at the best knows in the end the triumph of high achievement, and who at the worst, if he fails, at least fails while daring greatly.[3]

When we fall short or fail—regardless of how we may or may not have contributed to our failure—our resilience will enable us to remain strong in spirit and allow us to grow in wisdom.

Finally, building our resilience doesn't happen overnight. This process is not like a high school diploma where once we earn it, our classes end and we're proud alumni. There will surely be setbacks on our journeys toward increased resilience, sometimes caused by things outside of our control. Working on these resilience characteristics is a lifelong journey because the habits and people that help us cope, adapt, and transform will evolve throughout time, situation, and location. Throughout our lives, we can consistently develop the characteristics of resilience, learn how to adapt them to the circumstances, discover and rediscover practices and people that

---

3. Roosevelt, "Citizenship," para. 7.

are helpful, and maintain a spirit of agility and openness as we continually work to move to a place of increased resilience and peace.

THE ROLE OF FORGIVENESS

Being willing to forgive ourselves for our perceived shortcomings or mistakes and working toward forgiving others for being hurtful to us are essential components of resilience. They can't be understated and truly undergird each characteristic of resilience. For many, many years, I harbored a huge amount of responsibility and shame for my Coast Guard resignation. For a final paper for a seminary class about confession and forgiveness that I took in 2001, my professor tasked me with writing an autobiography using the material from the class to reflect on my own life experience. I shared my Coast Guard story. When I received the graded paper, I saw the professor's handwritten note, which said, "I found so much in here that you should celebrate about yourself. I also think you still accept more than your share of responsibility for things that were done *to* you, not by you." I read this note over and over with tears in my eyes. It was the first time I was able to relinquish even a small bit of my shame and responsibility and begin to forgive *myself*. Over the past twenty years, I have continued to wrestle with this idea. This reflection and reframing helped prepare me for an unexpected call from my friend Erica last June.

Erica was invited to be on a panel about resilience at the Service Academy Global Summit, an annual gathering of alumni of the five service academies. One of the other panelists, a beloved and popular talk-show host, was unable to attend, and she was calling to see if I might be willing to fill in at the last minute. She added, "Oh, and it's not an academic panel. The facilitator wants us to speak about our own personal issues related to resilience." Flying to Washington, DC, at the last minute seemed impossible because of childcare issues and work coverage, but far more intimidating was the prospect of speaking on a panel with actual war heroes and career military officers. The Divine intervened as I recalled part of a recent conversation with a trusted clergywoman friend Deb, who shared this with me: "My new goal is to take more risks and to say 'yes' more often." So I adopted her goal as my own and said yes.

I flew to DC and slept on Erica's couch after spending *hours* working on my four-minute speech. I delivered that speech the next afternoon and ended with this: "So this is not a heroic story. Mine is a story of how things fell apart, how *I* fell apart, and how the gifts and skills and strength within and around me helped me rebuild." When I finished, I felt flushed and was grateful my little part was over. I thoroughly enjoyed hearing the other panelists' stories of resilience and bravery. After each of us panelists shared, the audience—mostly high-ranking, male-identified military officers—proceeded to ask the most heart-felt, earnest questions to each of us, disclosing their own painful stories and sharing their own setbacks and challenges. The gathering of people gave a standing ovation at the end of the panel. After it concluded, the panel facilitator—a go-getting, spirited, female, retired Air Force brigadier general—marched up to me and pointed a finger at me, similar to the way that my executive officer pointed his finger to shame and blame me twenty years prior, and she said with certainty and firmness, "You *are* a hero." She then gave me a hug that was full of compassion, grace, and affirmation—a hug that helped swallow up years of my shame and regret.

This was another significant and healing step toward forgiving myself for the ways I contributed to the circumstances that led to my resignation and that hurt the people I loved. I have also been on a journey of forgiving the Coast Guard and those within it that contributed to my pain. Although it took time and intention, I am now deeply grateful for the Coast Guard Academy and the Coast Guard, in general. I am thankful for the strength I discovered, the friends I made, the incredible adventures I experienced, and the deep pride I felt for being part of something important. I am also truly appreciative for the ways the Coast Guard has been trying to learn its past and improve for the future, particularly in terms of issues related to sexism, racism, and homophobia. The joys and the struggles during my time in the Coast Guard helped me recognize my gifts, identify my "growing edges," and grow in strength, wisdom, and grit. Identifying, researching, and articulating these characteristics of resilience has been a rich and meaningful journey for me. For some (perhaps many) of us, this journey of resilience must begin with forgiveness, and being mindful of the characteristics of resilience and working to develop them throughout our lives will allow us to identify and celebrate our hopes and ideals and will motivate us to endure and to be transformed by hardship.

PERSONALIZING OUR STRATEGIES

Even in our challenges, traumas, failures, and disappointments, we are unique, beautiful people who have more strength than we realize. The strategies we employ to develop our resilience will be unique to each one of us. I invite you to look at these different characteristics, to personalize them with prayer and intentionality, and to discern if there are additional characteristics that you might benefit from including. Although I provided some generic questions for reflection in each chapter, here are some specific examples of questions I might ask myself related to the Seven Ps of resilience that take into consideration unique circumstances where we might find ourselves:

- *For parents*: Of what networks of support at my school or community am I a part? How am I role modeling positivity for my children? How well do I handle unexpected changes in the presence of my kids? How might my kids characterize my level of flexibility? How am I teaching problem-solving skills when my kids bump up against challenges instead of fixing their problems for them? How am I recognizing their abilities and inviting them to take more responsibility? What resources am I taking advantage of to learn and grow as an individual and as a parent? How am I providing them the values and beliefs of a spiritual or religious framework? How am I helping them keep a healthy perspective about entitlement, privilege, and equity? How do I discourage them from giving up easily or reward them for sticking with something that is challenging to them?

- *For college students*: Which of my friends are nonjudgmental, loving, and supportive? Which professors or staff members share my interests and might like to connect? What are my existing resources and areas of privilege? What can I do to make the transitions back and forth from home to school smoother? How intentional am I about the strategies and plans I am making for myself to achieve my short- and long-term professional and personal goals? What gives me deep joy and fulfillment? How clearly am I communicating with my family and the career center about what I feel passionate about, even if it differs from their expectations or plans for me? How am I staying connected with my sources of spiritual support while away from home or finding new ways to connect spiritually while away at school? How am I taking care of myself with regard to exercise, substance use, healthy eating, and sleep?

- *For those grieving*: Where am I finding nonjudgmental, caring support? Upon which faith communities, groups, or individuals can I rely for meals, support, or assistance? Which social contexts now feel uncomfortable for me, and in which contexts do I feel most supported? How am I celebrating and remembering the qualities of my loved one? What aspects of my life needs to change in terms of my role and responsibilities? How could I enlist help with those items? Which rituals or events need to be modified? How has my sense of purpose changed as a result of my loss, particularly if I have been the caregiver of my loved one? Which of my spiritual or religious beliefs are helpful, inspiration, or comforting? What am I doing to take care of myself such as sleeping well, eating, and staying active?

- *For older adults*: As friends move or pass away, how am I staying connected socially with people who love and appreciate me? How am I sharing the story of my life with others? What might I want to include in an ethical living will, and whose help can I enlist to create one? How well am I adapting to changes related to my work life, residential situation, and more? What changes might I anticipate, and how can I be best prepared for them? How can I ensure that my living will is clear and comprehensive, and how can I ensure the medical power of attorney I have named understands my wishes? How am I redefining my purpose as I transition from employment to retirement? What can I do to remember and celebrate the good moments of life such as sorting through my belongings and mementos and detailing the emotional or financial value of special items, while discarding old items that are weighing me down? What am I doing to stay healthy physically, spiritually, and emotionally?

- *For those engaged in social justice work*: Who am I collaborating with, and how are we supporting each other? How do I recognize and celebrate occasions of victory? How intentional is my strategy or plan? How am I defining my sense of purpose and my definition of success? What can I do to be sure I stay connected with that sense of purpose? How am I finding a balance between being informed about the issues and not being overwhelmed with the realities of them? How am

I ensuring that I do not take on too much responsibility to the point that it is hurting my spirit? How am I taking care of myself?

- *For educators*: How am I encouraging students to connect with each other in meaningful ways? How do I work to be kind to my students and affirm their efforts? How am I sometimes spontaneous and stray from the routine when it seems appropriate? How do I encourage problem-solving skills and publically recognize resourceful problem solving? When can I journal about the highlights of my days or keep notes of gratitude that I receive from students to remind me of my purpose? How am I taking care of myself emotionally or spiritually? What can I do to be sure I am setting good boundaries between my home and work life?

These lists are far from exhaustive but are examples of the kinds of questions we can ask ourselves as we work to be more mindful of these important characteristics of resilience. I invite you to make a list for yourself.

LET'S GET STARTED!

As you work to develop the characteristics of resilience, remember that you are stronger than you realize! When the circumstances seem dire, the strength of your body, mind, and spirit will enable you to stay focused on these characteristics of resilience—people, positivity, pliability, problem solving, purpose, piety, and perseverance—and will enable you to trust in your abilities to endure and to be transformed. Today is a great time to start this new chapter. In the words of Sensei Wu from *The Lego Ninjago Movie*, "We cannot change the past, but we can improve for the future."[4] Let's get started!

4. Logan et al., *Lego Ninjago*.

Bibliography

Ackerman, Courtney. "How Can Positive Psychology Help in the Treatment of Depression?" Positive Psychology Program, December 23, 2016, https://positivepsychologyprogram.com/positive-psychology-depression/.

Adam, David. "Meditation 'Leads to Longer Life.'" *Guardian*, May 2, 2005. https://www.theguardian.com/uk/2005/may/02/health.science.

Adams Helminski, Camille. *Rumi Daylight: A Daybook of Spiritual Guidance*. Boston: Shambhala, 1994.

Agulanna, Christopher. "Community and Human Well-Being in an African Culture." *TRAMES: A Journal of the Humanities & Social Sciences* 14:3 (September 2010) 282–98. http://kirj.ee/public/trames_pdf/2010/issue_3/trames-2010-3-282-297.pdf.

Akhtar, Salman, and Glenda Wrenn. "The Biopsychosocial Miracle of Human Resilience." In *The Unbroken Soul: Tragedy, Trauma, and Resilience*, edited by Henri Parens et al., 1–19. Lanham, MD: Rowan and Littlefield, 2008.

Al-Anon Family Groups. "How Can I Help My Problem Drinker Quit Drinking?" https://al-anon.org/newcomers/how-can-i-help-my/.

"American College Health Association-National College Health Assessment II: Undergraduate Student Data Report Spring 2018." Silver Spring, MD: American College Health Association, 2018. https://www.acha.org/documents/ncha/NCHA-II_Spring_2018_Undergraduate_Reference_Group_Data_Report.pdf.

Anderson, Dave. "Three Traits Veterans Bring to the Workplace." *Work of Honor*. https://www.workofhonor.com/news/company-stories/three-traits-veterans-bring-workplace.

Angelou, Maya. "The Distinguished Annie Clark Tanner Lecture." Lecture, Weber State University, Ogden, UT, May 8, 1997. https://awpc.cattcenter.iastate.edu/2017/03/21/the-distinguished-annie-clark-tanner-lecture-may-8-1997/.

———. *I Know Why the Caged Bird Sings*. New York: Random House, 2009.

Aquino, Corazon. Speech, Mount St. Vincent College, New York, 1984.

Barron, Carrier. "Creativity, Happiness and Your Own Two Hands." *Psychology Today*, May 3, 2012. https://www.psychologytoday.com/us/blog/the-creativity-cure/201205/creativity-happiness-and-your-own-two-hands.

"Basics of Buddhism." PBS. https://www.pbs.org/edens/thailand/buddhism.htm.

Baumeister, Roy, et al. "Bad Is Stronger than Good." *Review of General Psychology* 5:4 (2001) 323–70. http://assets.csom.umn.edu/assets/71516.pdf.

Benard, Bonnie. "Fostering Resiliency in Kids: Protective Factors in the Family, School, and Community." Portland, OR: Western Regional Center for Drug-Free Schools and Communities, August 1991. https://files.eric.ed.gov/fulltext/ED335781.pdf.

"Biography." Seussville.com. http://www.seussville.com/#/author.

Błażek, Magdalena, and Tomasz Besta. "Self-Concept Clarity and Religious Orientations: Prediction of Purpose in Life and Self-Esteem." *Journal of Religion & Health* 51:3 (2012) 947–60.

Bonhoeffer, Dietrich. *Prisoner for God: Letters and Papers from Prison.* Edited by Eberhard Bethge, translated by Reginald H. Fuller. New York: Macmillan, 1961.

"The Book No One Would Publish." DelaneyPlace.com, April 17, 2015. https://delanceyplace.com/view-archives.php?p=3565.

Borkovec, Thomas D., et al. "Preliminary Exploration of Worry, Some Characteristics and Processes." *Behaviour Research and Therapy* 21:1 (1983) 9–16.

Boyden, Jo, and Gillian Mann. "Children's Risk, Resilience, and Coping in Extreme Situations." In *Handbook for Working with Children and Youth: Pathways to Resilience across Cultures and Contexts*, edited by Michael Ungar, 3–25. Thousand Oaks, CA: Sage, 2005.

Brafford, Anne, and Martha Knudson. "Building Resilience and Grit: Adding to Your Emotional Intelligence Toolkit." Workshop, Association of Corporate Council Annual Meeting, Washington, DC, October 17, 2017.

Breslin, Michael J., and Christopher Alan Lewis. "Theoretical Models of the Nature of Prayer and Health: A Review." *Mental Health, Religion & Culture* 11:1 (2008) 9–21.

Bridges, William, *Transitions: Making Sense of Life's Changes.* Cambridge, MA: De Capo, 2004.

Brodwin, Erin. "The Thai Cave Football Coach Taught His Team to Meditate to Help Them through 17-Day Ordeal, Reports Say." *Independent*, July 11, 2018. https://www.independent.co.uk/news/world/asia/thai-cave-rescue-meditation-football-ekapol-chanthawong-a8441851.html.

Brown, Brené. *Rising Strong.* New York: Spiegel & Grau, 2015.

Buechner, Frederick. *Wishful Thinking: A Theological ABC.* New York: Harper One, 1993.

Burk, Domyo. "Changing Reality with Positive Thinking." *Bright Way Zen* (blog), February 14, 2012. https://brightwayzen.org/changing-reality-with-positive-thinking/.

Buscaglia, Leo. *Born for Love: Reflections on Loving.* New York: Fawcett, 1992.

Cabot, James Elliot. *A Memoir of Ralph Waldo Emerson.* Vol. 2. Cambridge: Riverside, 1887. https://archive.org/details/memoirofralphwal02cabo/page/488.

Cacioppo, John T. "Build Your Social Resilience." *Psychology Today*, March 6, 2010. https://www.psychologytoday.com/blog/connections/201003/build-your-social-resilience.

"Calvin on Vocation." *Every Square Inch* (blog), July 10, 2009. http://everysquareinch.blogspot.com/2009/07/john-calvin-on-vocation.html.

Capretto, Lisa. "Brené Brown on Self-Criticism, Judgment and the Power of Compassion." *Huffington Post*, February 25, 2014. https://www.huffingtonpost.com/2014/02/25/brene-brown-self-criticism-compassion_n_4848895.html.

Carey, Benedict. "Expert on Mental Illness Reveals Her Own Fight." *New York Times*, June 23, 2011. https://www.nytimes.com/2011/06/23/health/23lives.html.

Chavez, Mark. "The Decline of American Religion?" ARDA Guiding Paper Series. State College, PA: Association of Religion Data Archives, Pennsylvania State University, 2011. http://www.thearda.com/rrh/papers/guidingpapers/Chaves.pdf.

Chinonye, Onyeagba Joseph. "Igbo Proverbs, Idioms and Parables." IgboGuide.com. https://www.igboguide.org/guests/igbo-proverbs.htm.

Churchill, Winston. *My Early Life: 1874–1904*. New York: Touchstone, 1958.

Cognitive Behavior Therapy Los Angeles. "Problem-Solving Therapy." http://cogbtherapy.com/problem-solving-therapy-los-angeles/.

Craft, Lynette, and Frank M. Perna. "The Benefits of Exercise for the Clinically Depressed." *Primary Care Companion to the Journal of Clinical Psychiatry* 6:3 (2004) 104–11. https://www.ncbi.nlm.nih.gov/pmc/articles/PMC474733/.

Dalai Lama and Howard Cutler. *The Art of Happiness: A Handbook for Living*. New York: Riverhead, 1998.

"Dalai Lama on Analytic Meditation and How It Helps Cultivate Positivity." Central Tibetan Administration, January 30, 2017. https://tibet.net/2017/02/dalai-lama-on-analytic-meditation-and-how-it-helps-cultivate-positivity/.

Das, Ajit K. "Frankl and the Realm of Meaning." *Journal of Humanistic Education & Development* 36:4 (1998) 199–211.

Davey, Melissa. "The Most Dangerous Time: Five Women Tell Their Stories of Leaving an Abusive Relationship." *Guardian*, June 1, 2015. https://www.theguardian.com/society/ng-interactive/2015/jun/02/domestic-violence-five-women-tell-their-stories-of-leaving-the-most-dangerous-time.

David, Noah. "Why Waiting Is Hard." *Huffington Post*, August 1, 2014. https://www.huffingtonpost.com/2014/08/01/short-attention-span-waiting-hard_n_5621690.html.

Dervic, Kanita, et al. "Religious Affiliation and Suicide Attempt." *American Journal of Psychiatry* 161:12 (2004) 2303–8. https://ajp.psychiatryonline.org/doi/10.1176/appi.ajp.161.12.2303.

Doyle, Glennon. "Why the World Needs the Mentally Different." *Momastery* (blog), April 13, 2015. https://momastery.com/blog/2015/04/13/world-mentally/.

Edwards, Leonard. "Mentors Crucial to Curb Recidivism for Youths." *Juvenile Justice Information Exchange*, July 31, 2017. http://jjie.org/2017/07/31/mentors-crucial-to-curb-recidivism-for-youths/.

Elijah, A. M. "Can I Learn to Invent?" *Invention Intelligence* 8:8 (August 1973).

"Flexibility." Ahlul Bayt Digital Islamic Library Project. https://www.al-islam.org/secrets-success-ayatullah-mirza-jafar-subhani/flexibility.

Fontaine, Rodrigue. "Problem Solving: An Islamic Management Approach." Abstract. *Cross Cultural Management: An International Journal* 15:3 (July 2008) 264–74. https://www.emeraldinsight.com/doi/abs/10.1108/13527600810892549.

"'Football Gave Me Courage.'" Video. BBC News, August 19, 2016. https://www.bbc.com/news/av/world-asia-india-36684704/football-gave-me-courage.

Frankenberg, Elizabeth, et al. "Education, Vulnerability, and Resilience After a Natural Disaster." *Ecology & Society* 18:2 (2013) 189–201.

Frankl, Victor. *Man's Search for Meaning*. Boston: Beacon, 2006.

The Freedom Church. Interpretive sign, Middletown Heritage Trail, Middletown, CT.

Garcia, Sandra. "The Woman Who Created #MeToo Long before Hashtags." *New York Times*, October 20, 2017. https://www.nytimes.com/2017/10/20/us/me-too-movement-tarana-burke.html.

Garmenzy, Norman. "Reflections and Commentary on Risk, Resilience, and Development." In *Stress, Risk, and Resilience in Children and Adolescents: Processes,*

Mechanisms, and Interventions, edited by Robert Haggerty et al., 1–18. New York: Cambridge University Press, 1994.

Geisel, Theodor. *Oh, the Places You'll Go!* New York: Random House, 1990.

General Service Office. "Estimated Worldwide A.A. Individual and Group Membership." New York: Alcoholics Anonymous General Service Office, May 2018. https://www.aa.org/assets/en_US/smf-132_en.pdf.

The Golden Rule. Poster. Dayton, OH: Pflaum, 2000.

Goldfine, Rebecca. "Bowdoin Hires New Director of Spiritual Life." *Bowdoin Daily Sun*, January 24, 2013. https://dailysun.bowdoin.edu/2013/01/bowdoin-hires-new-director-of-spiritual-life/.

Goldman, Robert, and Stephen Papson. *Nike Culture: The Sign of the Swoosh.* Thousand Oaks, CA: Sage, 1998.

Goldstein, Carly, et al. "Current Perspectives on the Use of Meditation to Reduce Blood Pressure." *International Journal of Hypertension*, March 5, 2012, article 578397. https://www.ncbi.nlm.nih.gov/pmc/articles/PMC3303565/.

Greenberg, Melanie. "Worst Mistakes Parents Make When Talking to Kids." *Psychology Today*, September 18, 2012. https://www.psychologytoday.com/blog/the-mindful-self-express/201209/worst-mistakes-parents-make-when-talking-kids.

Grenville-Cleave, Bridget. *Positive Psychology: A Practical Guide.* New York: MJF, 2012.

Guindon, Mary H., and Fred J. Hanna. "Coincidence, Happenstance, Serendipity, Fate, or the Hand of God: Case Studies in Synchronicity." *Career Development Quarterly* 50:3 (March 2002) 195–208.

Hales, Craig, et al. "Prevalence of Obesity among Adults and Youth, United States, 2015–2016." Hyattsville, MD: National Center for Health Statistics, 2017. https://www.cdc.gov/nchs/data/databriefs/db288.pdf.

Hanford, Emily. "Angela Duckworth and the Research on 'Grit.'" Documentary transcript. American Public Media. http://americanradioworks.publicradio.org/features/tomorrows-college/grit/angela-duckworth-grit.html.

Harper, Ida Husted. *The Life and Work of Susan B. Anthony: Including Public Addresses, Her Own Letters and Many from Her Contemporaries during Fifty Years.* Vol. 2. Indianapolis: Bowen-Merrill, 1898. https://archive.org/details/lifeworkofsusanb02harp_0/page/n9.

Harris, Rorie N., et al. "BUDS Candidate Success through RTC: First Watch Results." Millington, TN: Bureau of Naval Personnel, November 2006. http://www.dtic.mil/dtic/tr/fulltext/u2/a463049.pdf.

Heider, John. *The Tao of Leadership: Lao Tzu's Tao Te Ching Adapted for a New Age.* Atlanta: Humanics Limited, 1985.

Henry, Gary. "Story and Silence: Transcendence in the Work of Elie Wiesel." *The Life and Work of Wiesel*, PBS Lives and Lives and Legacies Film, 2002. https://www.pbs.org/eliewiesel/life/henry.html.

Herman, Lily. "How I Wrote 1,000 Articles during My Four Years at Wesleyan." *Wesleyan University Magazine*, September 7, 2018. http://magazine.wesleyan.edu/2018/09/07/how-i-wrote-1000-articles-during-my-four-years-at-wesleyan-by-lily-herman-16/.

Hillenbrand, Laura. *Unbroken: A World War II Story of Survival, Resilience, and Redemption.* New York: Random House, 2010.

Holt-Lunstad, Julianne, et al. "Advancing Social Connection as a Public Health Priority in the United States." *American Psychologist* 72:6 (2017) 517–30. https://www.apa.org/pubs/journals/releases/amp-amp0000103.pdf.

Iris. "Best Friends Get Brutally Honest about Their Bodies." Video. October 10, 2016. https://www.youtube.com/watch?v=LzT2ZzDXceg.

Iyer, Pico. "Woman of the Year: Cory Aquino Leads a Fairy-Tale Revolution, Then Surprises the World with Her Strength." *Time*, January 5, 1987. http://content.time.com/time/subscriber/article/0,33009,963185-9,00.html.

Jefferson, Thomas. Letter CXXX, to John Adams, April 8, 1816. In Vol. 4 of *Memoir, Correspondence, and Miscellanies: From the Papers of Thomas Jefferson*, edited by Thomas Jefferson Randolph. 2nd ed. Boston: Gray and Bowen, 1830. http://www.gutenberg.org/files/16784/16784-h/16784-h.htm#link2H_4_0130.

Johnson, Howard Agnew. *Studies in God's Methods of Training Workers*. New York: International Committee of Young Men's Christian Associations, 1900. https://books.google.com/books?id=7Ts3AAAAMAAJ&.

Johnston, Elinor D. "Credo." Poem, displayed in First Congregational Church of Old Lyme, Lyme, CT.

Kelly, Maura. "A Slow-Books Manifesto." *The Atlantic*, March 26, 2012. https://www.theatlantic.com/entertainment/archive/2012/03/a-slow-books-manifesto/254884/.

Khomami, Nadia. "#MeToo: How a Hashtag Became a Rallying Cry against Sexual Harassment." *Guardian*, October 20, 2017, https://www.theguardian.com/world/2017/oct/20/women-worldwide-use-hashtag-metoo-against-sexual-harassment.

King, Martin Luther, Jr. "Keep Moving from This Mountain." Speech, Spelman College, Atlanta, GA, April 11, 1960.

———. "Loving Your Enemies." Sermon, Dexter Avenue Baptist Church, Montgomery, AL, December 25, 1957.

Koenig, Harold. *Is Religion Good for Your Health?: The Effects of Religion on Physical and Mental Health*. Binghamton, NY: Haworth, 1997.

Krakauer, Jon. *Into Thin Air: A Personal Account of the Mount Everest Disaster*. New York: Anchor, 1998.

Kreager, Derek A., et al. "Women's Education, Marital Violence, and Divorce: A Social Exchange Perspective." *Journal of Marriage and the Family* 75:3 (2013) 565–81. https://www.ncbi.nlm.nih.gov/pmc/articles/PMC3864686/.

Kushner, Harold. *When All You've Ever Wanted Isn't Enough: The Search for a Life That Matters*. New York: Pocket, 1986.

———. *When Bad Things Happen to Good People*. New York: Schocken, 1981.

Lewis, C. S. *The Great Divorce: A Dream*. New York: Harper Collins, 2002.

Lincoln, Abraham. Letter to John T. Stuart, January 23, 1841. In Vol. 1 of *Collected Works of Abraham Lincoln*, edited by Roy P. Basler, 229–30. Ann Arbor: University of Michigan Digital Library Production Services, 2001. https://quod.lib.umich.edu/l/lincoln/lincoln1/1:248?rgn=div1;view=fulltext.

"Lincoln Family Timeline." Abraham Lincoln Online. http://www.abrahamlincolnonline.org/lincoln/education/timeline.htm.

Lipka, Michael, and Claire Gecewicz. "More Americans Now Say They're Spiritual but Not Religious." *Fact Tank*, Pew Research Center, September 6, 2017. http://www.pewresearch.org/fact-tank/2017/09/06/more-americans-now-say-theyre-spiritual-but-not-religious/.

Logan, Bob, et al., screenwriters. *The Lego Ninjago Movie*. Directed by Charlie Bean. Burbank, CA: Warner Bros. Family Entertainment, 2017.

Lopez, Gomez, et al. "Comparing the Acceptability of a Positive Psychology Intervention versus a Cognitive Behavioural Therapy for Clinical Depression." *Clinical Psychology & Psychotherapy* 24:5 (2017) 1029–39.

MacDonald, Pat. "Laughter—The Best Medicine?" *Practice Nurse* 36:2 (2008) 38–39.

Marcus Aurelius. *The Meditations of Marcus Aurelius*. Book 4. Translated by George Long. 1862. MIT Internet Classics Archives. http://classics.mit.edu/Antoninus/meditations.4.four.html.

"Marine Accident Brief, Accident No. DCA-97-MM-033." Washington, DC: National Transportation Safety Board, December 30, 1999. https://www.ntsb.gov/investigations/AccidentReports/Reports/MAB9901.pdf.

Mark, Joshua. "Heraclitus of Ephesus." *Ancient History Encyclopedia*, July 14, 2010. https://www.ancient.eu/Heraclitus_of_Ephesos/.

Marshall, Stephen. "Lessons from the SEALs: Doing the Impossible." *The Man's Life* (blog), January 2, 2018. https://www.themanslife.com/2018/01/lessons-from-the-seals-doing-the-impossible/.

"Martha Washington Biography." Biography.com, April 2, 2014. https://www.biography.com/people/martha-washington-9524817.

Maxwell, John C. *The 21 Irrefutable Laws of Leadership*. Nashville: Thomas Nelson, 2007.

"Maya Angelou: In Her Own Words." BBC News, May 28, 2014. https://www.bbc.com/news/world-us-canada-27610770.

McArdle, Terence. "'Night of Terror': The Suffragists Who Were Beaten and Tortured for Seeking the Vote." *Washington Post*, November 10, 2017. https://www.washingtonpost.com/news/retropolis/wp/2017/11/10/night-of-terror-the-suffragists-who-were-beaten-and-tortured-for-seeking-the-vote/.

McCain, John. *Faith of My Fathers: A Family Memoir*. New York: Random House, 2016.

———. "John McCain, Prisoner of War: A First-Person Account." *U.S. News and World Report*, January 28, 2008. https://www.usnews.com/news/articles/2008/01/28/john-mccain-prisoner-of-war-a-first-person-account.

Meacham, Jon. "The End of Christian America." *Newsweek*, April 3, 2009. http://www.newsweek.com/meacham-end-christian-america-77125.

Melvill, Henry. "Partaking in Other Men's Sins." Delivered June 12, 1855. Sermon no. 2,365 in vol. 2 of *The Golden Lectures: Forty-Five Sermons Delivered at St. Margaret's Church, Lothbury, on Tuesday Mornings, from January 2, to December 18, 1855*. The Preacher in Print, 2nd ser. London: James Paul, 1856. https://books.google.com/books?id=lt8EAAAAQAAJ.

Mercurio, Zach. "Think Millennials Are Purpose Driven? Meet Generation Z." *Huffington Post*, November 28, 2017. https://www.huffingtonpost.com/entry/think-millennials-are-purpose-driven-meet-generation_us_5a1da9f3e4b04f26e4ba9499.

Mills, Kim. "The Truth about Cats and Dogs: Pets Are Good for Mental Health of 'Everyday People.'" American Psychological Association, July 11, 2011. http://www.apa.org/news/press/releases/2011/07/cats-dogs.aspx.

Ming-Dao, Deng. *Each Journey Begins with a Single Step: The Taoist Book of Life*. Newburyport: Hampton Roads, 2018.

Mogahed, Yasmin. Facebook post, March 5, 2013. https://www.facebook.com/YMogahed/posts/your-life-is-nothing-more-than-a-love-story-between-you-and-god-nothing-more-eve/589604111066915/.

Mooney, Margarita. "What Does It Mean to Live a Broken Life, Beautifully?" Workshop, Princeton Theological Seminary Women in Ministry Conference, Princeton, NJ, October 25, 2017.

Morse, Katherine. "Overcoming Adversity." Speech, Strong Girls Gala for Girls on the Run of NOVA, Clifton, VA, September 28, 2017.

Mujū. *101 Zen Stories*. Compiled by Nyogen Senzaki. 1919.

Nhat Hanh, Thich. *Fear: Essential Wisdom for Getting through the Storm*. San Francisco: HarperOne, 2012.

———. *Touching Peace*. Berkley, CA: Parallax, 2009.

———. "Watering Our Good Seeds." Dharma talk delivered at Plum Village, Loubès-Bernac, France, n.d. http://www.mindfulnessnyc.org/index_files/watering_our_good_seeds.htm.

Nietzsche, Friedrich Wilhelm. *Twilight of the Idols: Or, How to Philosophise with the Hammer*. In vol. 16 of *The Complete Works of Friedrich Nietzsche*, translated by Anthony M. Ludovici, edited by Oscar Levy, 1–121. New York: Macmillan, 1911. https://babel.hathitrust.org/cgi/pt?id=njp.32101068982022;view=1up;seq=13.

Nishioka, Rodger, and Dominique Robinson. "Resilience and Joy: Helping Adolescents Bounce Back in the Face of Adversity." Live-streamed lecture, Yale Youth Ministry Institute, Yale Divinity School, New Haven, CT, February 3, 2016.

Nouwen, Henry. *The Wounded Healer: Ministry in Contemporary Society*. New York: Image, 1979.

"Obituary: Cardinal Jaime Sin." BBC News, June 21, 2005. http://news.bbc.co.uk/2/hi/asia-pacific/4113534.stm.

"Obituary: Nelson Rolihlahla Mandela." Government of South Africa. http://www.mandela.gov.za/obituary.html.

Okere, Theophilus. *Philosophy, Culture and Society in Africa*. Nsukka: Afro-Orbis, 2005.

Ong, Czarina. "Louis Zamperini's Son Shares Details of His Father's Faith That Did Not Make It to *Unbroken* Film." *Christianity Today*, March 31, 2015. https://www.christiantoday.com/article/louis-zamperinis-son-shares-details-of-his-fathers-faith-that-did-not-make-it-to-unbroken-film/51085.htm.

"Overweight & Obesity Statistics." NIH National Institute of Diabetes and Digestive and Kidney Diseases. https://www.niddk.nih.gov/health-information/health-statistics/overweight-obesity.

Pennock, Seph Fontane. "Positive Psychology 1504: Harvard's Groundbreaking Course." Positive Psychology Program, June 16, 2015. https://positivepsychologyprogram.com/harvard-positive-psychology-course-1504/.

Peterson, Richard. *Women, Work, and Divorce*. Albany: SUNY Press, 1989. https://books.google.com/books?id=dtJ3uQ3objAC&.

Pinker, Susan. "The Secret to Living Longer May Be Your Social Life." Speech, TED conference, April 2017. https://www.ted.com/talks/susan_pinker_the_secret_to_living_longer_may_be_your_social_life.

Polletta, Francesca, and James M. Jasper. "Collective Identity and Social Movements." *Annual Review of Sociology* 27 (2001) 283–305. https://www.annualreviews.org/doi/pdf/10.1146/annurev.soc.27.1.283.

"Read Rachael Denhollander's Victim Statement against Larry Nassar." *Sojourners*, January 26, 2018. https://sojo.net/articles/read-rachael-denhollander-s-victim-statement-against-larry-nassar.

"Refugee Soccer Star: From Afghanistan to US." Video. BBC News, September 27, 2017. https://www.bbc.com/news/av/world-us-canada-41391605/refugee-soccer-star-from-afghanistan-to-us.

Rehmani, Nadia Amin. "Debating the Term Ummah as a Religious or Social and Political Notion," *Hamdard Islamicus* 33:1 (2010) 7–19.

Revuluri, Sindhumathi. "How to Overcome Impostor Syndrome." *Chronicle of Higher Education*, October 4, 2018. https://www.chronicle.com/article/How-to-Overcome-Impostor/244700/.

Riccobon, Rob. Speech, West Hartford Aquatics Team banquet, Farmington, CT, May 6, 2018.

Rogers, Fred. "Address by Fred Rogers." Commencement speech, Marquette University, Milwaukee, 2001. https://www.marquette.edu/universityhonors/speakers-rogers.shtml.

Roosevelt, Theodore. "Citizenship in a Republic." Speech, Paris, France, April 23, 1910. http://www.theodore-roosevelt.com/trsorbonnespeech.html.

Rubin, Gretchen. "The Eight Splendid Truths of Happiness." *Gretchen Rubin* (blog), November 30, 2011. https://gretchenrubin.com/2011/11/the-eight-splendid-truths-of-happiness/.

Rumi, Jalal Al-Din. *The Soul of Rumi: A New Collection of Ecstatic Poems*. Translated by Coleman Barks. New York: HarperOne, 2001.

Sacchetti, Andrea. Retirement speech, Fire House on Fort Mason, San Francisco, CA, February 19, 2016.

Sagor, Richard. "Building Resiliency in Students." *Educational Leadership* 54:1 (1996) 38–43. http://www.ascd.org/publications/educational-leadership/sept96/vol54/num01/Building-Resiliency-in-Students.aspx.

Sandberg, Sheryl. "Sheryl Sandberg on Why Women Need Mentors." Video address. LeanIn.org. https://leanin.org/education/mentorship-matters.

Schaper, Donna. "Scattered by Persecution." In *Watch: 2017 Advent Devotional*. Cleveland: United Church of Christ, 2017.

Schnitker, Sarah, and Robert Emmons. "Patience as a Virtue: Religious and Psychological Perspectives." In vol. 18 of *Research in the Social Scientific Study of Religion*, edited by Ralph Piedmont, 177–208. Leiden: Brill, 2007. https://books.google.com/books?id=JE2SnNF96ogC.

Sicinski, Adam. "Practical Ideas to Help You Overcome Worry and Regain Peace of Mind." *IQ Matrix* (blog). https://blog.iqmatrix.com/overcome-worry.

Smedes, Louis. *The Art of Forgiving*. New York: Ballantine, 1997.

Smith, Christian, and Patricia Snell. *Souls in Transition: The Religious and Spiritual Lives of Young Adults*. New York: Oxford University Press, 2009.

Sockolov, Matthew. "The Importance of Sangha in Buddhism." *One Mind Dharma* (blog), December 1, 2015. https://oneminddharma.com/sangha/.

Souers, Kristin. *Fostering Resilient Learners: Strategies for Creating a Trauma-Sensitive Classroom*. Alexandria, VA: Association for Supervision and Curriculum Development, 2016.

Southwick, Steven. "Promoting Resilience: Review of Evidence-Informed Factors." Lecture, Yale Divinity School, New Haven, CT, October 26, 2015.

Southwick, Steven, and Dennis Charney. *Resilience: The Science of Mastering Life's Greatest Challenges*. New York: Cambridge University Press, 2012.

Spear, Wayne K. "Nelson Mandela's Genius Was in His Patient, Flexible Pragmatism." *National Post*, June 28, 2013. http://nationalpost.com/opinion/wayne-k-spear-nelson-mandelas-genius-was-in-his-patient-flexible-pragmatism.

Sprint. "Stickin' It to the Man." Advertisement video, August 13, 2008. https://www.youtube.com/watch?v=ZG-VB5xb6KM.

Sreenivasan, Shoba, and Linda Weinberger. "Self-Blame: How Do You Respond When Things Go Wrong?" *Psychology Today*, January 1, 2018. https://www.psychologytoday.com/us/blog/emotional-nourishment/201801/self-blame-how-do-you-respond-when-things-go-wrong.

Stein, Jacob, et al. "Traumatization, Loneliness, and Suicidal Ideation among Former Prisoners of War: A Longitudinally Assessed Sequential Mediation Model." *Frontiers in Psychiatry* 8, December 12, 2017, article 281. https://www.ncbi.nlm.nih.gov/pmc/articles/PMC5732953/pdf/fpsyt-08-00281.pdf.

Stern, Stephen, et al. "Potential Benefits of Canine Companionship for Military Veterans with Posttraumatic Stress Disorder (PTSD)." *Society & Animals* 21:6 (2013) 568–81. https://www.animalsandsociety.org/human-animal-studies/society-and-animals-journal/articles-on-animal-assisted-activities/potential-benefits-canine-companionship-military-veterans-posttraumatic-stress-disorder/.

Stone, Lucy. "The Progress of Fifty Years." Speech, Congress of Women at the World's Columbian Exposition, Chicago, IL, 1893. http://womenshistory.info/progress-fifty-years/.

Stone Zander, Rosamund, and Benjamin Zander. *The Art of Possibility: Transforming Professional and Personal Life.* New York: Penguin, 2002.

"Suicide Rates Rising across the U.S." Centers for Disease Control and Prevention, June 7, 2018. https://www.cdc.gov/media/releases/2018/p0607-suicide-prevention.html.

"There Is a Balm in Gilead." African-American spiritual. http://www.hymntime.com/tch/htm/t/i/s/tisabalm.htm.

Thompson, Chris, and Meredith Thompson. "Seize the Day." Track 6 on the album *Clearwater*. Alkali Records, 2002. https://www.cmthompson.com/lyrics.html.

Truth, Sojourner. *The Narrative of Sojourner Truth.* Edited by Olive Gilbert. Boston: J. B. Yerrinton, 1850. https://digital.library.upenn.edu/women/truth/1850/1850.html#1.

Valentine, Matt. "6 Awesome Zen Stories That Will Teach You Important Life Lessons." *Buddhaimonia* (blog). https://buddhaimonia.com/blog/zen-stories-important-life-lessons.

Vecsey, George. "Norman Vincent Peale, Preacher of Gospel Optimism, Dies at 95." *New York Times*, December 26, 1993. https://archive.nytimes.com/query.nytimes.com/gst/fullpage-980CE7DB123FF935A15751C1A965958260.html.

Versluis, Anke, et al. "Reducing Worry and Subjective Health Complaints: A Randomized Trial of an Internet-Delivered Worry Postponement Intervention." *British Journal of Health Psychology* 21:2 (2016) 318–35.

Walesh, Stuart. "Using the Power of Habits to Work Smarter." *Helping You Engineer Your Future.com* (blog). http://www.helpingyouengineeryourfuture.com/habits-work-smarter.htm.

Wang, Wendy. "The Link between a College Education and a Lasting Marriage." *Fact Tank*, Pew Research Center, December 4, 2015. http://www.pewresearch.org/fact-tank/2015/12/04/education-and-marriage/.

Warren, Rick. *The Purpose Driven Life: What on Earth Am I Here For?* Grand Rapids: Zondervan, 2012.

Washington, Martha. Letter to Mercy Otis Warren, December 26, 1789. Maine Historical Society, Portland. http://marthawashington.us/items/show/25.

Weinberg, Melissa K., et al. "Sleep Well Feel Well: An Investigation into the Protective Value of Sleep Quality on Subjective Well-Being." *Australian Journal of Psychology* 68:2 (2016) 91–97.

Werner, Emmy. "Protective Factors and Individual Resilience." In *Handbook of Early Childhood Intervention*, edited by Samuel Meisels and Jack Shonkoff, 97–116. New York: Cambridge University Press, 1990.

West, Jane. *The Loyalists: An Historical Novel.* Vol. 3. London: Longman, Hurst, Rees, Orme, and Brown, 1812. https://archive.org/details/loyalistshistorio3west/page/n7.

Wiesel, Elie. "Oprah Talks to Elie Wiesel." Interview by Oprah Winfrey. *O* (magazine), November 2000. http://www.oprah.com/omagazine/oprah-interviews-elie-wiesel/.

——. *Night.* New York: Avon, 1960.

Williams, Caroline. "How Much Shut-Eye Do I Need?" *New Scientist*, June 2017, 109–10.

Williams, Ray. "Is Gen Y Becoming the New 'Lost Generation'?" LinkedIn Pulse, July 13, 2014. https://www.linkedin.com/pulse/20140713132101–1011572-is-gen-y-becoming-the-new-lost-generation.

Winerip, Michael. "Mulberry Street May Fade, but 'Mulberry Street' Shines On." *New York Times*, January 29, 2012. https://www.nytimes.com/2012/01/30/education/dr-seuss-book-mulberry-street-turns-75.html.

Wong, Paul T. P. "Meaning Therapy: Assessments and Interventions." *Existential Analysis: Journal of the Society for Existential Analysis* 26:1 (2015) 154–67.

Wuthnow, Robert. *After the Baby Boomers: How Twenty- and Thirty-Somethings Are Shaping the Future of American Religion.* Princeton, NJ: Princeton University Press, 2007.

Yancey, Philip. *What's So Amazing about Grace?* Grand Rapids: Zondervan, 1997.

Yeginsu, Ceylan. "U.K. Appoints a Minister for Loneliness." *New York Times*, January 17, 2018. https://www.nytimes.com/2018/01/17/world/europe/uk-britain-loneliness.html.

Made in the USA
Middletown, DE
03 January 2020